GW00870341

The Wisdom of Java

Ahmad Dzikran

Ahmad Dzikran

ISBN:1530814650
ISBN-13:9781530814657

DEDICATION

To my wife Wenny Agustina, and my son Kayvan

Ahmad Dzikran

Table of Contents

Ahmad Dzikran

ACKNOWLEDGMENTS

To all who helped me finishing this book : Aki Azied,
Djoyohusodo, My Grand Father, and Ni Mas,
THANK YOU VERY MUCH!

ABOUT THE COVER

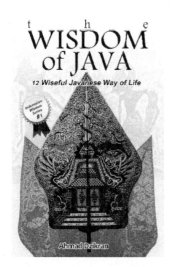

Gunungan (mountain) wayang is a triangle-like shaped leather puppet (*Wayang Kulit*) along with their contents. In it bottom part, there is a picture of the gate (palace's gate) guarded by two giant holding a sword and shield. In the Javanese *Wayang Kulit* show, *Gunungan* played or used as a palace. On the top part of Gunungan there is a picture of a tree entwined by a dragon.

The *Gunungan* has three sides. The good (positive) side, the evil (negative) side, the shadow side. The over-all shape of the mountain (*Gunungan*), reveals at the base a number of steps leading up to two temple doors. On either side of the doors stand two Raksasas, giant gate keepers, who guard our spiritual temple. At the beginning of the performance, when the music begins to play, the Dalang (a man who operates all *wayang* characters and telling the story) symbolically opens the temple doors. And invites his audience to enter the magical world of *Wayang* where our perceptions will change.

Inside *Gunungan* there are also pictures of various animals in the forest. The whole picture depict the circumstances in the wilderness. In other word, *Gunungan* symbolises the state of the world and its contents. Before the *Wayang Kulit* played, *Gunungan* plugged in the centre of the stage, leaning slightly to the right, which means that the show play has not started yet, like the world without any kind of life. Once played, Gunungan revoked, and lined up on the right.

The conical shape of *Gunungan* symbolises human life, where the higher science and increasing age, humans should be ever more narrow (*golong gilig*) by unify the soul, feeling, thought, and deed (*manunggaling jiwa, rasa, karsa and karya*) in human lives. In short, human life is to go to the Above One (God).

The following is some explanation and meaning of the images inside *Gunungan* :

1. A Palace Gate and two guards named *Cingkoro Bolo Bolo* and *Upoto*. These two guards are the symbol of the human heart which are have two tendencies : evil and good. The shield and *godho* (Javanese traditional big hammer warfare) they hold can be interpreted as keeper of dark and light world.

2. Forest (trees) and the beast in the *Gunungan* are symbols of various human character.

3. The Trees that grow throughout the body and spread to the top of the *Gunungan* symbolizes all of human behavior and thought that should grow and move forward (dynamic), so it's useful for coloring the world and universe (*Urip iku obah, Obaho sing ngarah-arah*). The tree also symbolized that God has given shelter and protection for human life in this world.

4. The Bird in *Gunungan* symbolizing human beings should make the world and the universe beautiful spiritually and materially.

5. The Bull in *Gunungan* symbolizing human beings should be strong, agile, resilient and tough.

6. Monkeys in *Gunungan* symbolizing people that should be able to select and sort out right or wrong, sweet or bitter, as any smart monkey choose good fruit, ripe, and sweet. So hopefully we are in good and right act.

7. Tiger symbolizing human beings should be a leader for themselves, human should be able to act wisely and control their appetite to achieve a better life, being useful for themselves, others, and the universe. Because if humans unable to be a leader for themselves and unable to control themselves, it will have fatal consequences. And all will be perished, just like *Gunungan* when it reversed, then the red color shown.

8. Image of the giant head symbolises the greedy of human character in daily life. This bad character can transform humans into something very evil, as evil as satan.

9. Image of *Ilu ilu Banaspati* (a genie or demon) on the back of a Gunungan symbolizes that life in this world has many temptations, trials, challenges and dangers that would come at any time threaten human safety.

10. Image of the ocean on *Gunungan* was symbolic of the human mind.

11. Image of a *joglo* House (*gapuran*) was symbolic of a house or a country that there is secure, serene, and happy life inside it.

Many meaningful symbols in every instruments and characters in Javanese puppet show (*Wayang Kulit*) Because the purpose of the show is basically to call people to improve themselves and willing to learn from his mistake. Because life is a learning process in itself.

OPENING WORDS

This ebook contains the wisdom views of life that taught by our ancestors in Java, Indonesia. This wisdom view has become Javanese way of life in the past, and indeed it still relevant for today.

But the wave of modernity and globalization have eroded many traditional views that actually very meaningful and wiseful. The view that can guide us in this life is a view based on wisdom and prudence, not only based on modernity and wealth.

The values in this ebook will be beneficial for you and show you the right path in life, make your heart calmer, happier and more grateful.

The traditional philosophy of Javanese community must continue to be studied, read, and disseminated throughout the community, so that the wisdom values will not lost in time. Therefore, I present to you all: **The Wisdom of Java.**

SHORT HISTORY OF JAVANESE

The Javanese are Indonesia's largest ethnic group and the world's third-largest Muslim ethnic group, following Arabs and Bengalis. "Wong Djawa" or "Tijang Djawi" are the names that the Javanese use to refer to themselves. The Indonesian term for the Javanese is "Orang Djawa" (The Javanese) The term *djawa* has been traced to the Sanskrit word *yava*, "barley, grain." The name is of great antiquity and appears in Ptolemy's *Geography.*

Like most Indonesian ethnic groups, including the Sundanese of West Java, the Javanese are of Austronesian origins whose ancestors are thought to have originated in Taiwan, and migrated through the Philippines to reach Java between 1,500BC and 1,000BC.

The Javanese primarily occupy the provinces of East and Central Java, although there are also some Javanese on other Indonesian islands. Java, one of the largest islands of Indonesia, is located between 6° and 9° S and 105° and 115° E. The climate is tropical, with a dry season from March to September and a wet season from September to March. Mountains and plateaus are somewhat cooler than the lowlands.

EARLY JAVANESE KINGDOMS

The island's exceptional fertility allowed the development of an intensive *sawah* (wet rice) agriculture, which in turn required close cooperation between villages. Out of village alliances, small kingdoms developed, including that of King Purnawarman of Taruma, but the first major principality was that of King Sanjaya, who founded the Mataram kingdom at the beginning of the 8th century. Mataram's religion centred on the Hindu god Shiva, and produced some of Java's earliest Hindu temples on the Dieng Plateau.

The Sailendra dynasty followed, overseeing Buddhism's heyday and the building of Borobudur. But Hinduism and Buddhism continued to coexist and the massive Hindu Prambanan complex was constructed within a century of Borobudur.

Mataram eventually fell, perhaps at the hands of the Sumatra-based Sriwijaya kingdom, which invaded Java in the 11th century. However, Javanese power began its revival in 1019 under King Airlangga, a semi-legendary figure who formed the first royal link between the island and Bali. Despite his role as a unifier, Airlangga later split the kingdom between his two sons, creating Janggala to the east and Kediri to the west.

It was only a matter of time before the balance of power was to change once again. Early in the 13th century the commoner Ken Angrok usurped the throne of Singosari (a part of the Janggala kingdom), defeated Kediri and brought Janggala under his control. The new kingdom ended in 1292 with the murder of its last king, Kertanegara, but in its short 70 years Javanese culture flourished and some of the island's most striking temples were built. Shivaism and Buddhism evolved during this time into the new religion Shiva-Buddhism, which is still worshipped in Java and Bali today.

MAJAPAHIT KINGDOM

The fall of the Singosari kingdom made room for one of Java's most famous early kingdoms, the Majapahit kingdom. Ruling from its capital at Trowulan, it established the first Javanese commercial empire by taking control of ports and shipping lanes. Its rulers skilfully brokered trading relations with Cambodia, Siam, Burma and Vietnam – and even sent missions to China – and claimed sovereignty over the entire Indonesian archipelago (which probably amounted to Java, Madura and Bali).

As the Majapahit kingdom went into decline in the late 1300s, Islam moved to fill the vacuum.

ISLAMIC KINGDOMS

Islam broke over Java like a wave, converting many among the island's elite, and by the 15th and 16th centuries the Islamic kingdoms such as Demak, Cirebon and Banten were on the ascent.

The Muslim state of Demak was the first to make military inroads into Java, raiding much of East Java and forcing many Hindu-Buddhists eastwards to Bali. Some, however, stayed put; the Tenggerese people of Bromo can trace their history back to Majapahit. Soon Demak was flexing its muscles in West Java, and in 1524 it took the port of Banten and then Sunda Kelapa (now Jakarta), before later overrunning Cirebon.

Demak's rule was not to last long. By the end of the 16th century the Muslim kingdom of Mataram had risen to take control of huge swathes of Central and East Java. Banten still remained independent, however, and grew to become a powerful maritime capital holding sway over much of West Java. By the 17th century, Mataram and Banten were the only two powers in Java left to face the arrival of the Dutch.

DUTCH PERIOD

As the Dutch set up camp in what was to become Jakarta, Banten remained a powerful ruling house and a harbour for foreign competitors. An impressive trading network was set up under Banten's greatest ruler, Sultan Agung, but unfortunately civil war within the house led to Dutch intervention and its eventual collapse.

The Mataram kingdom was another matter. As the power of the Dutch grew, the empire began to disintegrate, and by the 18th century infighting was taking its toll. The first two Javanese Wars of Succession were fought but fortunately resolved by the treaty of 1743; the ruler Pakubuwono II was restored to his battered court, but the price of concessions to the colonial power was high.

Obviously needing a fresh start, Pakubuwono II abandoned his old capital at Kartosuro and established a new court at Solo. However, rivalry within the court soon reared its ugly head again, resulting in the Third Javanese War of Succession in 1746. The Dutch rapidly lost patience and split the kingdom in three, creating the royal houses of Solo and Yogyakarta, and the smaller domain of Mangkunegaran within Solo.

Yogyakarta's founder, Hamengkubuwono I, was a most able ruler, but within 40 years of his death his successor had all but soured relations with the Dutch and his rivals in Solo. In 1812 European troops, supported by the sultan's ambitious brother and Mangkunegara, plundered the court of Yogyakarta and the sultan was exiled to Penang, to be replaced by his son.

Into this turbulent picture stepped one of the most famous figures of Indonesian history, Prince Pangeran Diponegoro, who subsequently launched the anti-Dutch Java War of 1825–30. At the end of this guerrilla war, the Dutch held sway over all the royal courts, which soon became ritual establishments with a Dutch *residen* (head of a residency during colonial administration) exercising control. With no real room or will for political manoeuvre, the courts turned their energies to traditional court ceremonies and artistic patronage, thus creating the rich cultural cities we see today.

JAVA TODAY

Java still rules the roost when it comes to political and economic life in Indonesia. It has the bulk of the country's industry, is easily the most developed island in Indonesia, and has over the years received the lion's share of foreign investment.

That doesn't mean it comes up smelling of roses, though. The economic crisis of the late '90s hit hard, and huge numbers of urban workers lost their jobs. Rising prices have caused unrest across the island, and disturbances, although sporadic, have remained a constant threat. The year 1998 saw the worst riots in the country's recent history, with Chinese communities targeted in Solo and Jakarta.

In the current century, terrorist targeting of foreign investments in Jakarta and the Bali bombings of 2002 and 2005 have left Indonesia's leading island reeling. Tourism is struggling to survive, and the capture of suspected terrorist Muslim cleric Abu Bakar Ba'asyir from a Solo hospital in 2002, and the killing of Jemaah Islamiah member Azahari Husin in Batu in 2005, has raised questions about the island's links with radical Islam.

But as the seat of government and with the bulk of the nation's resources behind it, Java will also be one of the first islands to recover.

Ahmad Dzikran

1

LIVE IS LIT
(URIP IKU URUP)

Live Is Lit (*Urip Iku Urup*). Our life should give benefit to others around us, the greater benefit we can give, would be much better for us as well as for others. Although we gave small benefit to others, it still means something. And most importantly, we should not be the cause of someone's problems. If we can't help our neighbors, at least don't be a burden to them.

It have very deep philosophical meaning, that we were born in this world not to live alone and enjoy all the gifts from God for ourselvef. But we were born to care of others, to give each other, help each other with no hope of return. All ancient teachings and religions have long been taught about this, that we as social beings must mutually interacting positively and helping others unconditionally.

The benefits that we give are like a lit. Lit isn't mean heat that destroy anything, but as the light that always shines on every step of the man to the right path. Therefore our life should have more value we can give to others as a bright light that shows each step for us to walk toward the truth.

Don't make friends or people around you feeling sad, angry or disturbed, because it is not our nature as noble creature. If we do something wrong, it can be considered a reasonable error. But if the mistake was done repeatedly, it means that errors has become your character.

Let's live with useful benefits and keep each other, so that we could be useful for everyone.

Our core value of life is not merely 'connecting' and having good relation with others, but also 'sharing' and 'caring'. Sadness will be reduced if we can tell it to a friend, while happiness will be more burgeon when it shared too. This has been affirmed by our ancestors : Insert chapter one text here.

"The people most beloved to God are those who are most beneficial to the people. The most beloved deed to God is to make a someone happy, or to remove one of his troubles, or to forgive his debt, or to feed his hunger. Whoever swallows his anger, then God will conceal his faults. Whoever suppresses his rage, even though he could fulfill his anger if he wished, then God will secure his heart on the Day of Resurrection. Whoever walks with his brother regarding a need until he secures it for him, then God the Exalted will make his footing firm across the bridge on the day when the footings are shaken."

In addition, if we provide benefits to others, everything will return to us.

[And Said], "If you do good, yo do good for yourselves; and if you do evil, [you do it] to yourselves."

Our ancestors said, *"Whoever fulfilled the needs of his brother, God will fulfill his needs."*

"Whoever grants respite to someone in difficulty or alleviates him,

God will shade him on the Day of Resurrection when there is no shade but His."

After learning the virtue "becomes a useful person", the question is how do we become useful?

GIVE BENEFIT AND HAPPINESS BY BEING USEFUL TO OTHERS

All of us want to be useful to others in some way. We want to feel needed, competent — like we're making a difference, in some small way.

Here five steps to be more useful person for others :

1. *First Key to Become a Useful Person That is You Should Have a Will*

The key is your will to provide benefits to others. If you have money or possesions, you can help them with that. If you have knowledge, you can teach poor kids in your neighbourhood. Even if you only have spare time, you can make yourself useful.

But if you don't have a strong desire, neither you have much money or not, have spare time or not, you will never make yourself useful to others.

2. *Take Action Now*

Life is short, don't be selfish. Do not prevent you from doing good. Please act immediately. Here are a few things you can do to make yourself useful:

   a. **Share what you know:** Be open with people about your knowledge. Let people know that you have special skills and that you can help when they're in a difficulties. Lots of people know how to do things, but they didn't tell anyone else — which is about the same as not knowing it at all, since when their special skills are needed, nobody knows to ask them and whatever it is that needs doing doesn't get done (or gets done badly).

b. **Be confident in yourself:** Know that your knowledge or thought is needed and valuable — and that nobody's going to reject a helping hand in when they need it. When we lack of confidence, we make excuses for not helping, because we're afraid to put ourselves on the line. Useful people don't make excuses — they jump in and do things with the best of their ability.

c. **Solve the current problem:** Help people with the immediate problem they're facing, without questioning and judgment, and without worrying about the problems that lie down the road. In a moment of crisis, lend your efforts to resolve the crisis. Once the problem is solved, in a way that makes people stronger not weaker, you can offer your advice in the future or for your evaluation of the situation. Remember, neither you or them can fix the problem, the best you can do is offering some advice for avoiding those problems in the future.

d. **Giving willingly — even when it's your job:** We always remember (and seek out) the people who went "the extra mile" in helping us. We also remember (and try to avoid) the people who helped us grudgingly because they were forced to do it. Show through your actions that it's your pleasure to help — even when (maybe especially when) you're being paid for your time.

e. **Satisfy your own curiosity:** Look for every opportunity to help out as a chance to learn something new, to expand your own knowledge and competency.

f. **Listen to others:** People's inability to do something often causes them real emotional tension; listen to them, both to provide a shoulder and to know what they've tried and where they think they went wrong. This gives them an opportunity — and it shows that you assess their efforts. Think of how demeaning it is when you call customer service with a complex computer problem and they tell you to check if the power's on — it feels bad when the people helping us belittle our knowledge and assume we're too stupid to handle even basic problems.

g. **Don't take over:** It can be tempting to push someone out of the way and just do it yourself. This almost inevitably makes people feel bad. Whenever possible, work with them and show that you appreciate their expertise and their perspective on that task.

h. **Know when to stop:** Likewise, once an immediate problem is solved, turn it back over to the person you help. Chances are, they know what to do once they get past the tricky part — give them a chance to demonstrate their own ability and talent.

i. **Teach, don't tell:** As much as possible, explain what you're doing and why. Leave the people you help feel a little bit better informed and more capable to handle the problem if it arise again (or at least to identify it, if handling it is out of their abilities). Don't assume because you're an expert, you think you're the only one who can understand what to do. (At the same time, be sensitive to things that really are beyond all expertise — don't make

17

them feel dumb because they don't understand a word you're saying!)

j. Be sensitive to people's feelings and shortcomings: I've said this several different ways already, but it bears repeating — help people feel better about the situation, not worse. Know that when people need help, it strikes deep at their sense of individual pride and competence. Don't put them down in any way, and don't let them put themselves down.

k. Ask for help: Give other people a chance to shine in their areas of expertise by asking for their help when you need it. You don't have to be good at everything to be insanely useful — build the sharing of assistance into your relationships with other people by letting them be useful when they can.

l. Model is best practices: Show through your actions what it means to be open and available to help others. Be open about how you do things so that others can learn by emulating you.

m. Be reliable: Once you commit to helping someone out, follow it through. Never let yourself feel that because you're doing someone a favor, they have to accept it on your terms. This demonstrates that you have the power in the relationship and makes them feel even weaker and more vulnerable than they probably already do. It might get the job done in the end, but it won't make you insanely useful.

3. *Always Give Benefits, Make it Your Lifestyle*

If giving benefit has become your habit, then you have already started to become useful. If you do it occasionally or depending on your mood, then you have not become a useful person.

However, if doing some good things became your habit and lifestyle, then that is your personality and attitude.

4. *Boost Your Benefits*

Should it be improved? Of course, because according to our our traditional life view, it just not saying to be personally useful, but it was said : *"most beneficial to the people",* that mean you are challenged to be champion in goodness. You have to be of the most benefit to others. Not just giving benefit.

5. *Take the Benefits For You As Well*

One of the principles of our life as already mentioned at the beginning of this chapter : *[And Said], "If you do good, yo do good for yourselves; and if you do evil, [you do it] to yourselves.."* meaning that all the good that you do will come back on you. If you're easy to help people in your neighbourhood, surely someday they will willingly help you if you need anything.

But remember one thing: in order to do good things, do it wholeheartedly and without hope for reward. Even in the Holy Quran there is one verse that mentions the virtue to conceal your charity.

"If you disclose your charitable expenditures, they are good; but if you conceal them and give them to the poor, it is better for you, and He will remove from you some of your misdeeds [thereby]. And God , with what you do, is [fully] Acquainted," (Holy Quran, Soorah *Al Baqara* (The Cow), verses : 271)

Then doing good and be beneficial to others means you need to do it without publicity, unknown, and you don't tell it to anyone. You must be ready become a hidden hero : **unseen,**

but people can take the benefit from you.

Useful for others is a long-term savings, one day you'll get the reprisal from what you did before, as long as you are sincere.

"So whoever does an atom's weight of good will see it (good consequence)."

2

HUMANS LIVE IN THE WORLD SHOULD PURSUE SAFETY, HAPPINESS, AND WELL-BEING, AND ERADICATE THE NATURE OF INSOLENCE AND GREEDY (MEMAYU HAYUNING BAWANA, AMBRASTA DUR HANGKARA)

The Earth we live in have been created by God with full of perfection. Earth, with all its beautiful creatures is to be a peaceful, safe, and pleasant for the human. To human race, God has given His entrust the management of this planet. It is in our hands the responsibility to manage this planet carefully for our happiness and prosperity.

With abundant resources, the Earth can become a heavenly place to mankind. Everything we need, like delicious healthy food are in our range, various beauty places and other good things provided by Earth can sustain our happiness. And of course with all what has provided by the Earth, should be no one living in hunger and suffering. Because the Earth is very rich and completely enough to satisfy the needs of mankind.

All problems emerged in the life of mankind such as hunger, poverty, and suffer aren't because the Earth does not provide anything what human need, but it all happened as a result of human's greedy and their selfish acted. Human's greedy have created fundamental problems which should not be exist. Greed made some people unable to utilize various sources available on Earth, that led to a very big and deep life gap : some live with very luxurious while others live in poverty.

The presence of the wide economic gap between the poor and the rich can be described in the story below:

This life we can say as a banquet meal held by a wealthy King who was very popular with his generosity. The King invites whole people to attend the huge banquet. A wide variety of delicious food and drinks prepared to satisfy the entire people in his kingdom.

On the day of the banquet, all of food and drinks have been served at tables in the vast Empire square. All the people from any region and cities assembled at the banquet.

After King gave a speech, then he lets his people to enjoy a variety of dishes orderly. But something he doesn't expected happen, most people are tempted by delicious dishes couldn't control themselves and began to show greed. Their greed makes them unabashedly took various foods as many as they can without thinking of others. Some of them taking food and put into the bags for themselves.

Their greedy attitude that eventually triggered some others to do similar things. And finally the banquet event turned into a mass scramble for food. Everyone is scrambling to get as many as possible food on the tables. As a result, a lot of food being wasted, dirty, and downtrodden. Some people managed to get the food in an amount very much, while some others only managed to gain a little. There was a great disparity that caused misery for most people.

This is why I do not agree with one of capitalism principles : *laissez freire*. Because we have a dark potential to be greedy and selfish creatures.

Because of this principle, all abundant resources of Earth to support human life became insufficient to bring out prosperity the entire of human race.

Some people are more concerned about themself and ignoring other's interests. Human's greed has made this life run unbalanced. Greed caused enmity and hatred that eventually drag mankind to the brink of a prolonged suffer. The only way for humanity developing beautiful and prosperous life is to build a togetherness among them.

Forming a brotherhood that supported by affection among us is important key to regain harmony in our life. This will make the human race is capable to utilize all available resources for their prosperity.

Greed is the root of evil on the Earth. Greed is the main cause of human suffering and misery. It has risen all forms of exploitation around the world. And therefore to ensure this planet as a place of peaceful life, safe and pleasant for the human race, inevitability for us all to ensure the planet free from greed and wrath.

That's mean everyone carry big responsibility to fight greed, exploitation, and inequity in this world. Fight those things doesn't mean it should be done with violence, although sometimes violence also required to fight it. Violence should be the last step in the effort to free this world from greed, wrath, and injustice. But the first step is to build human awareness, educate people to be ready for sharing, caring, and working together, no matter colors, ethnics, and religions. Recall mankind to their humanity nature and ensure them to build life based on compassion. All races must realize the nature of their creation that placed us in a situation to achieve harmony, peace, and prosperity only by being unified and brothers.

WHY WE BECAME GREEDY?

You must have heard *Homo Homini Lupus* "Man is a wolf to man", a popular Roman proverb by Plautus (dead 184 B. C.) It is because human's greed, some people acted like wolves to others. Never care others as long as they can fulfill their interests, never listen to others while pursuing what they want. Get rid of anyone who considered can interfere their ambitions. This is the global character of modern humans: busy, full of ambition, and individualist.

This is extreme mode for craving the wealth. **The first type of craving for wealth** is that a person has extreme love for wealth and also relentlessly exerts efforts to attain it – via means which are lawful – being excessive in that, striving hard and making painstaking efforts and toiling in order to attain it.

It has been reported that this hadeeth was in response to the appearance of some elements of this, as at-Tabaraanee reports from `Aasim ibn `Adiyy, radiyallahu `anhu who said, 'I bought a hundred shares from the shares of Khaybar and that reached the Prophet Muhammad pbuh said, *"Two ravenous wolves remaining amongst sheep whose owner has lost them will not be more harmful than a Muslim's."*

There is nothing more to chasing after wealth than the wastage of a person's noble life for that which has no value. Instead he could have earned a high rank (in Paradise) and everlasting bliss, but he lost this due to his craving after provision – which had already been assured to him and allotted to him, and it was not possible for anything to come to him except what was decreed for him – then on top of this he does not benefit from that, but rather abandons it and leaves it for someone else.

He departs from that and leaves it behind so that he will be the one held accountable for it, yet someone else benefits from it. So in reality he is only gathering it, yet someone else benefits from it. So in reality he is only gathering it for someone who will not praise him for that, whilst he himself goes on to One who will not excuse him for that – this itself would indeed be enough to show the blameworthiness of this craving.

The person who has this craving behavior, wastes his valuable time and engages himself in that which is no benefit to himself – in journeying and exposing himself to dangers in order to amass that which will only benefit someone else, so it is as is said:

"So one who spends his days in gathering wealth –Out of fear of poverty – then he has achieved only poverty."

It was said to a wise man, *"So and so has amassed wealth,"* so he said, *"Then has he amassed days in which to spend it?"* It was said, *"No"* So he said, *"Then he has amassed nothing!"*

It was also said in some narrations from the People of the Book, *"Provision has already been allotted and the one greedy for wealth is deprived. Son of Aadam! If you spend your life in seeking after this world then when will you seek after the Hereafter?" "If you are unable to do good deeds in this world, then what will you do on the Day of Resurrection?"*

Ibn Mas'ood (a Prophet's companion) said, "Certain faith (*yaqeen*) is that you do not make the people happy by angering God, and that you do not envy anyone for that which God has provided, and that you do not blame anyone for something which God has not given you – since provision will not be brought on by a person craving after it, nor will it be repelled by a person's disliking it. Indeed God through His Justice has made joy and happiness dependent upon having certain faith and contentment, and He has made worries and sorrow spring from doubt and displeasure."

One of the predecessors said: "Since predecree is a reality then craving is futile. Since treachery exists in people's characters then trusting everybody is to expose oneself to humiliation. Since death awaits everybody, then being satisfied with this world is foolishness."

'Abdul-Waahid ibn Zayd (Islamic Scholar from Basra, Iraq. Died after 767 A.C). used to swear by God that a person's craving after this world was more fearful to him than his worst enemy. He also used to say, "O my brothers! Do not grow up craving after his riches and increase in earnings or wealth, rather look upon him with the eye of one of who detests that he is preoccupying himself with that which will cause his ruin tomorrow in the Place of Return – and is proud with that." He also used to say, "Craving has two types: Craving which is an affliction and craving which is beneficial. As for the craving which is beneficial, then it is one's desire for that which is obedience to God, and as for the craving which is an affliction – then it is a person's craving after this world."

Craving after this world torments a person, he is preoccupied and does not attain joy or pleasure whilst amassing – since he is preoccupied. He does not find time – due to his love of this world – for the Hereafter, and is preoccupied with that which will perish and forgets that which will abide and remain.

In this regard a person said,

"Do not envy a brother who craves after riches –rather look upon him with aversion.

Indeed the one who craves is preoccupied with his Wealth from having any happiness due to his belongings."

Someone else said in this regard:

"O gatherer and miserly one being watched closely by time which is wondering which of its doors it should be close.

You have gathered wealth, but think have you gathered for it O gatherer of wealth – days in which you can spend it.

Wealth is hoarded away with you for those who will inherit it. The wealth is not yours except on the day when you spend it.

Satisfaction is for the one who settles in its neighbourhood.

And in its shade he finds no worries to disturb him."

A wise person wrote to a brother of his who desired this world:

"To proceed, you have become one who craves after this world. It will serve you whilst taking you away from it with accidents, illnesses, calamities and infirmity. It is as if you have not seen one who craves prevented from what he desires, nor one who shuns this world granted provision, nor one who died despite having great wealth, nor one who is fully satisfied in this world with a small amount."

An unknown poem from our classic record rebuked a brother of his for covetousness, saying,

"O my brother you are a seeker and one sought. You are being sought by One whom you cannot escape, and you are seeking that for which you have been sufficed. O brother, it is as if you have not seen one who craves being prevented, nor one who shuns the world

being granted provision."

A wise man said,

"The people who have the greatest degree of restlessness are the envious, those who have the greatest degree of happiness are the contented. Those who

persevere most through suffering are those who are covetous. Those who have the simplest and most pleasant life are those who most strongly refuse this world. The one

who will suffer the greatest regret is the scholar whose actions contradict his knowledge."

The second type of craving after wealth is that in addition to what has been mentioned in the first type, he also seeks wealth through unlawful means and withholds people's rights – then this is definitely blameworthy greed and covetousness.

"And whoever is saved from his covetousness, such are those who are successful."

Avarice is eager craving which causes a person to take things which are not lawful for him, and to withhold the rights of others. Its reality is that a person craves that which God has forbidden and prohibited him from, and that one is not contented with the wealth and womenfolk and whatever else God has made lawful for him. So God, the Most High, has made lawful for us that which is good from foods, drinks, clothing and women and has forbidden us to acquire these things except by lawful means and He made lawful for us the blood and wealth of the Unbelievers and those fighting against us. He also forbade us from everything impure from foods, drinks, clothing and women, and He forbade us from seizing people's wealth and spilling their blood unjustly. So he who limits himself to that which is permitted for him is a Believer, and one who goes beyond that into what he has been forbidden – then this is a blameworthy avarice which is inconsistent with *Iman* (true faith in belief, word and action).

Therefore Javanese ancestors informed that avarice causes a person to cut off relations, commit sins and to be miserly – and miserliness is a person's clinging on greedily to what he has in his hand. Whereas avarice is seeking to obtain that which does not belong to him unjustly and wrongfully – whether it is wealth or something else. It is even said that it is the head of all sins.

It was said, "Avarice (*loba*) and *Iman* (True Belief) will not combine in the heart of a Believer."

The best of *Iman* is self-restraint and compliance/liberality (*kamirahan*)," Self-retraint here has been explained to be withholding oneself from forbidden things, and *kamirahan* as the carrying out of the obligatory actions. Also the word *loba* (avarice) may sometimes be used to mean *kikir* (miserliness) and vice-versa, however in origin they are different in miserliness meaning as we have mentioned.

If the person's craving after wealth reaches this level then the deficiency it causes in a person's believe is clear – since failing to fulfill what is obligatory and falling into what is forbidden reduce one's believe without a doubt to the point that nothing but a little remains of it.

CRAVING FOR STATUS

A person who craving after status is even more destructive than his craving after wealth. Seeking after worldly status, position, leadership and domination causes more harm to a person that his seeking after wealth – it is more damaging and harder to avoid since even wealth is expended in seeking after leadership and status.

Seeking status through authority, leadership, wealth, and this is very dangerous – since it will usually prevent a person from the good of the Hereafter and nobility and honour in the next life.

"That home of the Hereafter We shall assign to those who seek neither haughtiness nor any corruption on earth. The good end is for the pious."

One of the predecessor said, *" No one seeks after authority and then behaves justly in it.*

"Whoever loves wealth and status and fears adversity will not behave with justice."

"You will be keen to attain authority and it will be a source of regret on the Day of Resurrection. So what an excellent wet-nurse it is and what an evil weaner."

Know that craving after status and position inevitably causes great harm before its attainment due to the striving necessary to attain it, and also afterwards due to the person's strong desire to hold onto it which produces injustice, haughtiness and other evils.

Aboo Bakr al-Aajurree, who was one of the wise scholars and teachers at the start of the fourth century, wrote at treatise about the manners and the sentiments of the scholars and it is one of the best works on this topic. One who studies it will know from it the way of the scholars of the *Salaf* (predecessor), and will know the innovated ways contrary to their way. So he describes the evil scholar at length, from this description is that: 'He has become infatuated with love of this world, and with praise, honour and position with the people of this world. He uses knowledge as an adornment just as a beautiful woman adorns herself with jewellery for this world, but he does not adorn his knowledge with action upon it." He then mentions a lengthy speech and then says, "So these characteristics and their like predominate in the heart of one who does not benefit from knowledge, so whilst he carries these attributes his soul will come to have love of status and position – so that he loves to sit with kings and the sons of this world. The he loves to share in their opulent lifestyle, sharing their lavish attire, their comfortable transport, servants, fine clothing, delicate bedding and delicious food. He will love that people throng to his door, that his saying is listened to, and that he is obeyed – and he can only attain the latter by becoming a judge (*qaadee*) – so he seeks to become one. Then he is unable to attain it except at the expense of his religion, so he debases himself to the rulers and their helpers, serving them himself and giving them his wealth as a tribute. He remains silent when he sees their evil actions after entering their palaces and homes. Then on top of this he may praise their evil actions and declare them good due to some false interpretation in order to raise his position with them. So when he has accustomed himself to doing this over a long period of time and falsehood has taken root in him –then they appoint him to the position of judge (*qaadee*) and in so doing slaughter him without a knife."

"Verily, We sent (Messengers) to many nations before you (O Muhammad (pbuh). And We seized them with extreme poverty (or loss in wealth) and loss in health with calamities so that they might believe with humility," (soorah Al-An`aam [6]:42).

It also happened that one of the people of the past was a judge and he saw in a dream that someone was saying to him, "You are a judge and God is a Judge." So he awoke in a distressed state and removed himself from the position of a judge and abandoned it.

Some of the pious judges in centuries ago used to prevent the people from calling them 'Judge of judges' since this name resembles the name 'King of kings' which the Prophet Muhammad (pbuh) censured that one should use hyperbolic or revering words as a title, and 'Judge of judges' is like that.

Also related to this is the one having status and authority loves being praised and commended for his actions and seeks that from the people. Those who do not comply with this will end in suffer as a result. It may even be that his actions are actually more deserving of blame than of praise, or he manifests something that is apparently good – and loves to be praised for it, yet in reality he is intending something evil and is happy that he is able to deceive the people and fool them about it.

"Think not that those who rejoice in what they have done (or brought about), and love to be praised for what they have not done, think not that they are rescued from the torment, and for them is a painful torment."

Since this poem was write down regarding those who have these attributes, and this attribute (i.e. seeking praise from the creation and loving it and punishing those who do not give it) is not fitting except for God, alone, having no partner. This is why the rightly guided leaders used to forbid people to praise them for their actions and any good which if they did, and they would order that rather praise be given to God alone, having no partner – since all blessings are from Him.

`Umar ibn Abdul - `Azeez, was very particular about this and he once wrote a letter to be read out to the people performing Hajj. It contained an order that they should be treated well and that oppression of them should stop, and in it there occurred, *"And do not praise anyone for this except God, since if He abandoned me to my own devices I would be just like the others."*

Due to this, the just rulers and judges, never used a call to glorification themselves but rather to the glorification of God alone and that He is to be singled out with worship and divinity. From them were those who did not wish for leadership at all except as an aid to calling to God alone. Some of the righteous people who accepted the position of judge said, *"Indeed I accepted this in order to use it to help me in ordering the good and forbidding the evil."*

Indeed the Messengers and their followers would persevere in the face of injury and harm which they suffered whilst calling to God, and in carrying out God's commands they were put into the severest hardship by the people and yet they bore it with patience. Indeed being pleased with that, since one who has love may find pleasure in any harm he meets whilst seeking to please the one whom he loves. Just as `Abdul-Maalik ibn `Umar ibn `Abdul-Azeez used to say to his father when he was the *khaleefah* (Leader) and he had keen desire that the truth and justice be established, "O father I would have loved that we had been forced into boiling cooking pots for the sake of God the Mighty and Majestic, than i do unjust and contrary to the truth."

Another righteous person said, "I would have loved that my flesh were cut away with scissors if it meant that all the creation would obey God the Mighty and Majestic, life safely and feel the justice."

This saying of his was related to a certain wise person, so he said, "If what he was speaking of was sincere concern for the creation, otherwise I do not know." Then he fainted. The meaning of this is that the one who said this had true and sincere concern for the creation and pity for them, fearing God's punishment for them, so he would have loved that they could have been saved from God's punishment at the expense of his ownself. It could also be that he was considering the Majesty and Greatness of God and the glorification, honour, obedience and love due to Him, so he wished that the creation would fulfil that even if it meant the most severe harm to himself. This is the state of mind of the distinguished ones who love God and have knowledge of Him and keep Him in mind. This is what caused the man to faint.

God, the Most High, also described in His Book those who love Him as being those who fight Jihaad in His cause and do not fear the blame of those who seek to blame.

Concerning this someone said:

"I find that being blamed whilst pursuing what you desire is delightful, For having love for your remembrance let those who wish to blame me do so."

STAND AGAINST ALL GREED AND MALICE

Not only pursue their happiness and realize the existence of inequality, we should stand against any poverty, greed, and human domination over others as well.

Here are a few things you can do to build social justice and promoting the prosperity of humanity.

1. *Charity*

Inequality exists in all societies. Unfortunately, it has become one of the root causes of poverty for millions of disadvantaged people living across the globe. Victims of inequality in any society have limited access to basic necessities and resources such as education, healthcare, water and sanitation and housing.

Fighting inequality is about giving people their right to live with dignity and respect. Confronting inequality is ultimately a battle against poverty.

Charity, preached by every religion of the world, is a way of bringing justice to society. And justice is the essence of religion, Islam has therefore made charity that is *Zakah*, obligatory and binding upon all those who embrace the faith; it has been made into an institution in order to give in permanence and regularity.

A society can flourish only when its members do not spend all their wealth to fulfil their own desires but reserve a portion of it for parents, relatives, neighbors, the poor and the debilitated. As the saying goes: Charity begins at home. A true believer is thus always prepared, after meeting the needs of his family, to assist other people in need of his help.

Thus the spirit of kindness and well wishing is the essence of charity. The giver is not to expect any reward from the beneficiary as there awaits for him an abundant reward from God - material, moral and spiritual - what God deems it best to confer on His servant.

Charity should be lawfully earned or acquired by the giver. It should include such things as are of use and value to others.

"Charity is for those in need." This is general principle which enjoins us to help people in need, be they good or bad, on the right path or not, Muslims or non-Muslims. No one should judge in these matters. The foremost ends in charity should be God's pleasure and our own spiritual good. The concept of charity in Islam is thus linked with justice. It is not limited to the redressal of grievances. It implies apart from the removal of handicaps, the recognition of the right that every human being has to attain the fullness of life.

According to Islamic ethics, our joy and happiness are not complete unless we make our less fortunate brethren happy. It is a lesson worth remembering, especially in this era of materialism, when scant regard is paid to the moral and ethical values which are so much emphasised by religion.

Our children are taught nowadays that only the fittest has a right to survive, and weaklings are bound to perish. In this educational back-ground, why should they care if a poor man dies of hunger? He is a misfit, and he must perish.

But the teaching of religions is quite different. Religion teaches us to care; it enjoins the strong and wealthy to help their weak and poor brethren.

The Qur'an states: *'And be steadfast in your prayer and pay charity; whatever good you send forth for your future, you shall find it with God, for God is well aware of what you do'* (soorah Al Baqara [2]:110). Charity is central to a Muslim's life.

The best charity is to satisfy a hungry person, said Prophet Muhammad (pbuh). He also said *"No wealth (of a servant of God) is decreased because of charity."* (Al-Tirmidhi, Hadith No. 2247).

I am believe in the axiom "WE KNOW HOW TO MAKE MONEY BUT WE DO NOT KNOW WHO TO SPEND MONEY". We spend the first 20 to 30 years of our lives in acquiring skilled and marketable talents to earn money, but we are not taught how to spend money. We are not given guidance concerning financial transactions.

Charity is a way of God. Spending in the way of God *'fee Sabil God"* e.g. in Hajj, the poor, on widows and orphans or on relatives and friends to help them out. The Qur'an encourages the Muslim to donate their funds: *'the likeness of those who spend their wealth in the way of God, is as the likeness of a grain that sprouts seven spikes. In every spike there are 100 grains, and God multiplies for whom He will'* (soorah Al Baqara [2]: 261). Giving charity is thereby not seen as detracting from income, but rather as a multiplication in terms of spiritual observance. It is like one who sows a good grain of wheat in the field from which grows a plant on which sprout seven ears and each ear yields hundred grains. As a result, one grain was worth a total yield of 700 grains. When one spends in the way of God, he or she receives in return (reward in the Hereafter) on the scale of one to seven hundred.

How to get 700 grains out of one grain? This is possible only when the grain is good. The farmer is an expert in the art of farming. The soil for the grain should be good; we need to add fertilizer, water, and sunshine to the plant. One needs to prevent disease to the plant and also prevent the plant to be eaten by cattle, etc. Similarly that which is spent in the way of God should be clean, pure and *Halal* (lawful)- BECAUSE GOD ALMIGHTY ACCEPTS NOTHING EXCEPT WHAT IS CLEAN, PURE AND HALAL.

As in Islam, Christianity has emphasized that the charity is the highest form of love, signifying the reciprocal love between God and man that is made manifest in unselfish love of one's fellow men. St. Paul's classical description of charity is found in the New Testament (I Cor. 13). In Christian theology and ethics, charity (a translation of the Greek word *agapē*, also meaning "love") is most eloquently shown in the life, teachings, and death of Jesus Christ. St. Augustine summarized much of Christian thought about charity when he wrote: "Charity is a virtue which, when our affections are perfectly ordered, unites us to God, for by it we love him." Using this definition and others from the Christian tradition, the medieval theologians, especially St. Thomas Aquinas, placed charity in the context of the other Christian virtues and specified its role as "the foundation or root" of them all.

A common understanding of charity is what many people of faith would call 'almsgiving' - a strong tradition in both Christianity and Islam - as well as Buddhism and other faiths. During Lent, for example, Christians are urged to pray, to fast and to give alms (money or goods) to people in need. Motivation is important - in both Christianity and Islam giving alms in secret is better than receiving human praise for the practice.

Charity in Christianity is not just almsgiving, and should not be seen only as an obligation or duty. Charity is love. Christians believe that God's love and generosity towards humanity moves and inspires us to love and be generous in response.

Jesus taught that to love God and to love neighbour are the greatest commandments. Charity is not an optional extra, but an essential component of faith. In Matthew's Gospel (chapter 25), Jesus identifies himself with those who are poor and excluded, and teaches that we will be judged, not on how beautiful our altars are, but on the way that we treat others. We cannot profess to worship God in church, yet not express that love practically to our neighbour. And our neighbour is not just someone local to us. In the story of the Good Samaritan Jesus made clear that our neighbour may be someone on the other side of the world, who is not 'one of us' but different. Because of our common humanity - because we are each created and loved by God - we cannot allow anyone to go without what is needed for a dignified life.

The early saints of the Christian church had a very challenging view of charity. They argued that what God provides generously and freely is effectively 'stolen' by those who hoard their wealth instead of sharing what they have with those in need. A Christian understanding of charity is far more radical and demanding than simply giving from what we have 'left over'. Christians believe that anything that we have is a gift from God and does not belong exclusively to us. It must be shared if there is someone who needs it more.

Religious teachings about charity in line with the Javanese wisdom principles that all the wealth we have are not fully belong to us, all just an entrusted goods from God/gods that must be managed for the benefit of ourselves and others. Others in need should receive outpouring of affection from the rich, and not leave them.

Charity more than just giving, but it has to help the poors to expand their ability to get better live than before. If you give a charity to others, you can't just leave them. But you should aid them to increase their income with your charity, use it to develop new business or job, even just selling handkerchief.

In a big scale, you can organize charity program within a community, then begin to develop cheap or free housing program for homeless people in your city.

So, charity is an integrated action to help people, systematic steps to reduce poverty and inequality in this world. If many people do this with determination, day by day, poverty will perish from our civilization.

2. *Applying Justice*

In our worldview, justice denotes placing things in their rightful place. It also means giving others equal treatment. Justice is also a moral virtue and an attribute of human personality, as it is in the Western tradition. Justice is close to equality in the sense that it creates a state of equilibrium in the distribution of rights and duties, but they are not identical. Sometimes, justice is achieved through inequality, like in unequal distribution of wealth.

Treating people equally means that you treat them the same, regardless of their race, sex, social status or anything else. Treating people fairly means that you treat them in ways that are most appropriate to their needs. This may mean that you treat them differently than you treat others because they have different needs than others do.

It is important to treat people fairly and not discriminate against them as everybody is different and they should be treated as individuals.

Equal does not mean that we are all the same. Each of us is different in our own special way but we also have the common qualities that make us all humans. So each of us should be treated with respect and dignity and treat others in the same way.

Apply justice by treating others equally will prevent human being greedy, cheating, selfish, and giving priority to its own interests or group by oppressing interests of others.

3

ALL PERSEVERANCE, INSULAR, ANGER, CAN ONLY BE DEFEATED BY WISE ATTITUDE, GENTLE AND PATIENT
(SURA DIRA JAYANINGRAT, LEBUR DENING PANGASTUTI)

This aphorism is part of verse of a canto named "Sekar Kinanthi" in the "Witaradya" by R. Ngabehi Ranggawarsita (1802-1873 AD) from Kasunanan (minor Sultanate) Surakarta (now part of modern Solo, Central Java), which tells the story of R. Citrasoma, son of King Aji Pamasa in the country called Witaradya.

Complete version of "Sekar Kinanthi" are as follows:

Jagra angkara winangun

Sudira marjayeng westhi

Puwara kasuh kawasa

Sastraning jro Wedha muni

Sura dira jayaningrat

Lebur dening pangastuti

The free translation is as under:

Building of savagery has enforced

The braves won in many dangerous battles

Finally he couldn't resist the temptation of power

In the books of wisdom

It's told many brave and noble knight

Ruined by the throne

Verse 1 to 3 indicate a courage and invincible person who because of his and he never undefeated, eventually became ambitious to the thron. And when he was in power, he became totally despotic. Whereas verse 4 to 6 explain that according to the book of wisdom, the such nature can be defeated by tenderness.

Human's heart are very easy to change and corrupt. Many people who initially had the best quality, eventually ruined by a subtle hazards: power and money.

We are so aware of visible threats, but not alert enough to the unseen enemies. That is why many good people destroyed by the temptations, ambition, and lust. No matter right or wrong, all moral principles and ethics was violated for achieving personal ambitions.

When humans heart have been marred by unseen enemies, they instantly transformed into violent, brutal, full of anger, aggression, and despotic being. Human that originally was affectionate being, became so rude and unwilling to accept advice from others.

The rough, harshs, full of hatred and revenge souls have become features of modern humans now. Look, how many times we heard words like "mother fucker", "fuck you", "ass hole," and others? Or how many times you say it? If you often enough, please fix yourself, you may be a part of damaged human.

Where is human tenderness? Where all the compassionate attitude that replaced by hatred and anger?

The answer is that tenderness and loving attitude still exists deep in human's heart, but they were covered by dust and dirt.

FIGHTING ANGER, AGGRESSION, AND HATRED WITH PATIENCE

We can suppress anger and aggression, either way making things worse for ourselves and others. Or we can practice patience: wait, experience the anger and investigate its nature.

Ancient Javanese teachings tell us that patience is the antidote to anger and aggression. When we feel aggression in all its many forms—resentment, bitterness, being very critical, complaining and so forth—we can apply the different practices we've been given and all the good advice we've heard and given to other people. But those often don't seem to help us. That's why this teaching about patience caught my interest a few years ago, because it's so hard to know what to do when one feels anger and aggression.

At that point, patience means getting smart : to stop and wait. You also have to shut up, because if you say anything it's going to come out aggressively, even if you say, "I love you."

Patience has a lot to do with getting smart at that point and just waiting: not speaking or doing anything. On the other hand, it also means being completely and totally honest with yourself about the fact that you're furious. You're not suppressing anything— patience has nothing to do with suppression. In fact, it has everything to do with a gentle, honest relationship with yourself. If you wait and don't feed your discursive thought, you can be honest about the fact that you're angry. But at the same time you can continue to let go of the internal dialogue. In that dialogue you are blaming and criticizing, and then probably feeling guilty and beating yourself up for doing that. It's torturous, because you feel bad about being so angry at the same time that you really are extremely angry, and you can't drop it. It's painful to experience such awful confusion. Still, you just wait and remain patient with your confusion and the pain that comes with it.

Patience has a quality of enormous honesty in it, but it also has a quality of not escalating things, allowing a lot of space for the other person to speak, for the other person to express themselves, while you don't react, even though inside you are reacting. You let the words go and just be there.

This suggests that fearlessness goes with patience. If you practice the kind of patience that leads to the de-escalation of aggression and the cessation of suffering, you will be cultivating enormous courage. You will really get to know anger and how it breeds violent words and actions. You will see the whole thing without acting it out. When you practice patience, you're not repressing anger, you're just sitting there with it—going cold turkey with the aggression. As a result, you really get to know the energy of anger and you also get to know where it leads, even without going there.

You've expressed your anger so many times, you know where it will lead. The desire to say something mean, to gossip or slander, to complain—to just somehow get rid of that aggression—is like a tidal wave. But you realize that such actions don't get rid of the aggression; they escalate it. So instead you're patient, patient with yourself.

Developing patience and fearlessness means learning to sit still with the edginess of the energy. It's like sitting on a wild horse, or on a wild tiger that could eat you up. There's a limerick to that effect: "There was a young lady of Niger, who smiled as she rode on a tiger. They came back from the ride with the lady inside and the smile on the face of the tiger." Sitting with your discomfort feels like riding on that tiger, because it's so frightening.

When we examine this process we learn something very interesting: there is no resolution. The resolution that human beings seek comes from a tremendous misunderstanding. We think we can resolve everything! When we human beings feel powerful energy, we tend to be extremely uncomfortable until things are resolved in some kind of secure and comforting way, either on the side of yes or the side of no. Or the side of right or the side of wrong. Or the side of anything at all that we can hold on to.

But the practice we're doing gives us nothing to hold on to. Actually, the teachings themselves give us nothing to hold on to. In working with patience and fearlessness, we learn to be patient with the fact that we're human beings, that everyone who is born and dies from the beginning of time until the end of time is naturally going to want some kind of resolution to this edgy, moody energy. And there isn't any. The only resolution is temporary and just causes more suffering. We discover that as a matter of fact joy and happiness, peace, harmony and being at home with yourself and your world come from sitting still with the moodiness of the energy until it rises, dwells and passes away. The energy never resolves itself into something solid.

So all the while, we stay in the middle of the energy. The path of touching in on the inherent softness of the genuine heart is to sit still and be patient with that kind of energy. We don't have to criticize ourselves when we fail, even for a moment, because we're just completely typical human beings; the only thing that's unique about us is that we're brave enough to go into these things more deeply and explore beneath our surface reaction of trying to get solid ground under our feet.

Patience is an enormously wonderful and supportive and even magical practice. It's a way of completely changing the fundamental human habit of trying to resolve things by going either to the right or the left, calling things right or calling things wrong. It's the way to develop courage, the way to find out what life is really about.

Patience is also not ignoring. In fact, patience and curiosity go together. You wonder, Who am I? Who am I at the level of my neurotic patterns? Who am I at the level beyond birth and death? If you wish to look into the nature of your own being, you need to be inquisitive. The path is a journey of investigation, beginning to look more deeply at what's going on. The teachings give us a lot of suggestions about what we can look for, and the practices give us a lot of suggestions on how to look. Patience is one extremely helpful suggestion. Aggression, on the other hand, prevents us from looking: it puts a tight lid on our curiosity. Aggression is an energy that is determined to resolve the situation into a hard, solid, fixed pattern in which somebody wins and somebody loses.

When you begin to investigate, you notice for one thing, that whenever there is pain of any kind—the pain of aggression, grieving, loss, irritation, resentment, jealousy, indigestion, physical pain—if you really look into that, you can find out for yourself that behind the pain there is always something we are attached to. There is always something we're holding on to.

I say that with such confidence, but you have to find out for yourself whether this is really true. You can read about it: the first thing tat our ancestors ever taught was the truth that suffering comes from attachment. That's in the books. But when you discover it yourself, it goes a little deeper right away.

As soon as you discover that behind your pain is something you're holding on to, you are at a place that you will frequently experience on the spiritual path. After a while it seems like almost every moment of your life you're there, at a point where you realize, you are actually have a choice. You have a choice whether to open or close, whether to hold on or let go, whether to harden or soften.

That choice is presented to you again and again and again. For instance, you're feeling pain, you look deeply into it, and you notice that there's something very hard you're holding on to. And then you have a choice: you can let go of it, which basically means you connect with the softness behind all that hardness. Perhaps each one of us has made the discovery that behind all the hardness of resistance, stress, aggression and jealousy, there is enormous softness that we're trying to cover over. Aggression usually begins when someone hurts our feelings. The first response is very soft, but before we even notice what we're doing, we harden. So we can either let go and connect with that softness or we can continue to hold on, which means that the suffering will continue.

It requires enormous patience even to be curious enough to look, to investigate. And then when you realize you have a choice, and that there's actually something there that you're attached to, it requires great patience to keep going into it. Because you will want to go into denial, to shut down. You're going to say to yourself, "I don't want to see this." You'll be afraid, because even if you're starting to get close to it, the thought of letting go is usually very frightening. You may feel that you're going to die, or that something is going to die. And you will be right. If you let go, something will die. But it's something that needs to die and you will benefit greatly from its death.

The path of developing loving-kindness and compassion is to be patient with the fact that you're human and that you make these mistakes. That's more important than getting it right. It seems to work only if you're aspiring to give yourself a break, to lighten up, as you practice developing patience and other qualities such as generosity, discipline and insight. As with the rest of the teachings, you can't win and you can't lose. You don't get to just say, "Well, since I am never able to do it, I'm not going to try." You are never able to do it and still you try. And, interestingly enough, that adds up to something; it adds up to loving-kindness for yourself and for others. You look out your eyes and you see yourself wherever you go. You see all these people who are losing it, just like you do. Then, you see all these people who catch themselves and give you the gift of fearlessness. You say, "Oh wow, what a brave one—he caught by himself." You begin to appreciate even the slightest gesture of bravery on the part of others because you know it's not easy, and that inspires you tremendously. That's how we can really help each other.

First story is taken from Mahabharata epic, particularly in Barathayudha war scene between the Kurawa against the Pandawa. One day, the Kurawa sent out King Salya to fight against King Yudhistira from Pandawa.

King Salya, in his heart preferred to be with Pandawa, but he was trapped by Duryudana (oldest brother of the Kurawa) in such a way so that he had to join Kurawa. He fought with all his strength, he had a powerful mantra called 'CANDRA BIRAWA'.

When he spelled the mantra a lot of giants came out from his ears, and killed a lot of Pandawa's soldiers. Pandawa forces were deteriorated. Again, the wise Basudewa Kresna knew his secret. The only man who could face him was Yudhistira, considered as the holiest man of all the people. He was honest, kind-hearted, patience, and never lied.

The CANDRA BIRAWA giants, would not attack if they were not attacked first, they did only counter-attack. When King Salya spelled CANDRA BIRAWA, it was only one giant appeared, but if this giant was killed then he would became two life giants, two would became four and then sixteen, etc. They would multiply themselves to be hundreds and thousands of giants. The soldiers who were counter-attacked by CANDRA BIRAWA giants should be death definitely, their whole blood were sucked.

King Yudhistira was a man who did not like to fight, he should meet King Salya but instructed by Basudewa Kresna not to attack the CANDRA BIRAWA giants. The giants were confused, they did not know what to do in facing a passive man. The giants soon reduced their total numbers. From 1000 giants became 10 and then became 1, the original CANDRA BIRAWA giant.

The CANDRA BIRAWA went back into the ears of the owner. King Salya had to fight without the help of his spell, he was getting tired as he was an old man. When King Yudhistira released his heirloom JAMUS KALIMOSODO, King Salya had not enough power to defend himself, he got killed right away.

The Javanese traditional teachings (Kejawen) had a conclusion that only a honest and low-profile Knight like Yudhistira entitled to posses a holy mantra Kalimasada, the five principles to guide people (and society) to live in patience and honesty.

King Yudhistira faced his physically big and most powerful enemy by wait and still. He stands against anger with patience and won the battle!

In Christianity, we found patient character of Jesus in His work of salvation. The patience of Jesus Christ is seen in his relationships with people and in his perseverance through trial and suffering to death. Followers of Christ are called to demonstrate patience in all their relationships and circumstances.

An example from the life of Christ illustrates this. Jesus was very patient with his disciples. They were sometimes thickheaded, lazy, selfish, and slow to believe. Even from a merely human standpoint, we can see how frustrating they must have been. How much more irritating it would be for God Incarnate to interact daily with these men. In spite of Jesus' miracles and words of wisdom, they were focused upon themselves and wavered in their belief about who he really was. To say that was uncomfortable for Jesus would be an understatement. Yet do we find him railing at his disciples over their foolishness and stupidity? Or making fun of them when they make mistakes?

Occasionally he does remark that his disciples are slow to believe, or he asks rhetorically how long they will fail to have faith in him, but these are always appropriate reminders about just what was at stake for them. These were fitting and useful rebukes, not petty venting.

Notice that Jesus' refusal to complain about his irritating disciples can be described as an exercise of self-control. Surely he would have been justified in blistering them with insults. It's worth noting that his omniscience guaranteed that every possible joke and embarrassing remark was at his disposal on any particular occasion. This makes his self-control even more admirable.

The relentless tenderness of Jesus challenges us to give up our false faces, our petty conceits, our irritating vanities, our preposterous pretending, and become card-carrying members of the messy human community. Jesus calls us to be tender with each other because He is tender.

Even Jesus called all Christians to love their enemy, as said in Holy Bible, Matthew 5:43-45

43 "You have heard that it was said, 'YOU SHALL LOVE YOUR NEIGHBOR and hate your enemy.' 44 But I say to you, love your enemies and pray for those who persecute you, 45 so that you may be sons of your Father who is in heaven; for He causes His sun to rise on the evil and the good, and sends rain on the righteous and the unrighteous...."

When Jesus said we are to love our enemies, He was creating a new standard for relationships. He proclaimed to the crowds listening to His Sermon on the Mount that they knew they were to love their neighbor because the command to love our neighbor was a law of God (Leviticus 19:18). That we must therefore hate our enemy was an inference incorrectly drawn from it by the Jews. While no Bible verse explicitly says "hate your enemy," the Pharisees may have somewhat misapplied some of the Old Testament passages about hatred for God's enemies (Psalm 139:19-22; 140:9-11). But Jesus replaced this idea with an even higher standard: *"Love your enemies and pray for those who persecute you, that you may be sons of your Father in heaven"* (Matthew 5:44-45). Jesus goes on to explain that loving those who love us is easy and even unbelievers can do that. Then He commands us to *"be perfect, therefore, as your heavenly Father is perfect"* (Matthew 5:43-48).

Jesus explained to His followers that they should adhere to the real meaning of God's law by loving their enemies as well as their neighbors. A Pharisee once asked Jesus, "Who is my neighbor?"

(Luke 10:29). Jesus then told the Parable of the Good Samaritan. Here Jesus taught that His followers must demonstrate love to all kinds of people—no matter what faith, nationality, or personality—enemies included. If you love your enemies and "pray for those who persecute you," you then truly reveal that Jesus is Lord of your life. In short, Jesus gave wonderful example how to fight anger with tenderness.

By using an illustration of the sun rising and the rain falling on both the good and the evil, Jesus shows God's undiscriminating love to all people. His disciples then must reflect His character and exhibit this same undiscriminating love for both friends and enemies. Jesus is teaching us that we must live by a higher standard than what the world expects—a standard that is impossible for us to attain by our own efforts. It's only through the power of God's Spirit that His people can truly love and pray for those who intend to do them harm (Romans 12:14-21).

Another sample of tenderness and patience we can see in the holy prophet Muhammad (pbuh). Throughout the period of his mission, the Prophet Muhammad (pbuh) experienced all manner of difficulty. Deniers and polytheists, from among his own people, insulted him most terribly, even calling him a magician or a madman. Others wanted to kill him and even schemed to do so. Despite all that, the Prophet (pbuh) tried to teach people of all backgrounds and cultures about the Qur'an, and therefore about proper morality and good behavior.

At a very difficult time in his life, just after a period known as the Year of Sorrow, Prophet Muhammad went to the city of Taif hoping to find people who would listen and support his message to humanity. Instead of support he found insults and injuries. He was chased out of town. With his sandals filled with blood, from the injuries inflicted upon him by men, women and children throwing rocks, Prophet Muhammad prayed to God for help. In response, the Angel of the Mountains asked for the Prophet's permission to cause the mountains surrounding Taif to crumble, killing all of the city's inhabitants. Despite his pain and suffering, something he had every right to be angry about, the Prophet's reply was, *"No, for I hope that God will bring forth from their progeny people who will worship God Alone, and none besides Him."*

After ten years of living in Medina, ten years of teaching the people how to love and obey God, ten years of establishing a fair and equitable Islamic community, Prophet Muhammad and his followers were able to return to Mecca. His patience was at last rewarded yet he still rode in on a donkey with tens of thousands of followers. Prophet Muhammad could have thrown patience to the wind and exact a terrible vengeance. He did not! Mecca lay at his feet, enemies stood with heads bowed in surrender and Prophet Muhammad spoke by the mercy of his Creator and said, **"I speak to you in the same words as (Prophet) Yusuf (Joseph) spoke to his brothers. This day there is no reproof against you; Go your way, for you are free."**

At the time of the Prophet Muhammad (peace be upon him) lived a blind beggar Jew who cursed God's messenger and he said all the people that they did not listen to his exhortations, he is a liar! This old man was not familiar with the Prophet Muhammad (peace be upon him), but despite this did not stop swearing at him. When the news of the beggar Judah went to the messenger, he did not curse and swear at him, and he took the habit each day to visit the poor and feed. The prophet Muhammad (peace be upon him) was feeding the old man until't leave this world, and the beggar Jew even did not suspect that feeds him the man he hates. After the death of Muhammad (peace be upon him) poor Jew was waiting for him and wondered why he does not come good man and did not feed him?

When Abu Bakr (may God be pleased with him) heard about this act of the Prophet, he went to the market and found that very poor blind man and began to feed him, as the prophet Muhammad (peace be upon him) did. Then suddenly a Jew got angry and said, "Who are you?" Abu Bakr replied that he was the man who fed all these years. Beggar Jew replied, No! Do not lie to me! The man was so nice to hold hands, and the food he gave was very easy to chew, because he softened it to me..."

Upon hearing this, Abu Bakr could not resist and started to cry. After that, said, "The man who came to visit you all these years - was the Prophet Muhammad (peace be upon him), I'm one of his followers".

Beggar Jew could not recover from this and wondered how the Prophet Muhammad, whom he had so long covered the railing could be so generous to him? Jew said through tears that indeed there is no God but God, and Muhammad - his Prophet, and became a Muslim.

This is just one of the hundreds of stories that happened with our honorable Prophet Muhammad (peace be upon him). Sometimes people don't have patience and love towards others. Quarrel and burn the bridges is always easier, a Muslim should seek not easy, but right way. It's a good attitude, a kind word and even warm glance melt the heart of the one who shot an arrow of anger in the soul. Who knows, maybe that is what will cause that he will become a true Muslim.

Tales of King Yudhistira, Jesus Christ, and the Prophet Muhammad (pbuh) shows us that patience can lead man to achieve glory and triumph. They have been successful in their respective missions : Yudhistira managed to defeat King Salya, Jesus managed to spread the teachings of compassion in Christianity, and the Prophet Mohammed managed to hoist the banner of monotheism in the whole Arabian Peninsula only in 23 years.

Let us contemplate, why in this world we can see a lot of hatred, anger, murder, terror, and racism? And not all of it have to be solved with violence if we understood the root of the problem. Why many Muslims being terrorists, because they've seen the West as one of the great exponents of neo-colonialism, oppression, and exploitation. Then the leaders of the West must review their policies against third world countries, especially Islamic countries where Western leaders put them as a barn food for Western civilization supremacy.

Why racism still exist? Because most people feels that themselves or their culture are more superior than others. But there is no static culture, all culture and civilization are moving and changing : forward or backward. Is it our culture that we are proud of had moving forward or backward?

Because of that this world need an intensive dialogue between different cultures, so that there is no prejudice against other cultures or races. Dialogue can reduce prejudice, when prejudice is reduced, then any anger or hatred are reduced as well.

Ahmad Dzikran

4

STRUGGLING WITHOUT THE NEED TO BRING THE MASSES, WINNING WITHOUT DEGRADING OR HUMILIATING, AUTHORITATIVE WITHOUT RELYING ON POWER, RICH WITHOUT BASED ON POSSESIONS
(NGLURUK TANPA BALA, MENANG TANPA NGASORAKE, SEKTI TANPA AJI-AJI, SUGIH TANPA BANDHA)

What is the meaning of life when we are hated by others due to our own behavior? It seems pointless if we adore ourselves with all the worldly attributes such as power, wealth, physical appearance, if in fact we have no friends.

We also don't need to make others embarrassed or hurted just because we want to "revenge" on someone. It would be much more dignified, if we dare to forgive others, though they didn't want to admit their mistakes and did not want to make peace with us. The greatness of the soul is legible when we dare to confess and apologize; at the same time willing to forgive those who did wrong to us.

In this modern era, many people want to be appreciated and respected by others with strive to be rich, famous, handsome or beautiful, and if necessary be a leading man. Even while they are struggling to reach the top of success, they often hurting others, degrade competitors, and humiliate the opponent.

In politics for example, a candidate will attempt to reveal the disgrace and scandal of their political opponents to public so that public will deny to select them. Why? For what? Whether by dropping your political opponents would it be a guarantee that you will become a better leader?

Power, wealth, physical appearance, and popularity become the main requirement for us to be in top position in the community, respected and admired, even followed.

But those things are not eternal. When we are getting poor, old, no longer notable, people would leave us one by one. We will be dumped, alone, and seems we never existed.

A status symbol is a perceived visible, external denotation of one's social position and perceived indicator of economic or social status. Many luxury goods are often considered status symbols. Status symbol is also a sociological term – as part of social and sociological symbolic interactionism – relating to how individuals and groups interact and interpret various cultural symbols.

Why do some people do their best to show that they are rich or that they are wealthy? before you can understand why people show off their wealth, you need to know more about the dynamics of showing off.

WHY DO PEOPLE SHOW OFF?

People show off for various reasons but the most two common ones are:

> • **Showing off to prove something:** A person could show off his wealth in order to prove to people that he is rich. Sounds like a dumb statement right? In fact when you analyze this statement deeply you will find out that people who show off mistakenly assume that others look down upon them and that's why they show off to improve their position. So a person who shows off his wealth does it because he believes that others don't think that he is wealthy or even classy! (see also Why do people talk about themselves)

> • **Showing off to compensate:** In the solid self confidence program i said that many people show off to compensate for something that they believe they lack. For example a person could show off his wealth if he believes that others find him uninteresting. In such a case he is trying to fill the gap of being perceived as boring by showing that he is rich.

PEOPLE SHOW OFF THEIR WEALTH WHEN THEY AREN'T REALLY WEALTHY

People feel like talking about the things they achieved when they dont yet feel that they have reached the top. Once they reach the top they will act in a more humble way and will be less likely to show off unless they want to achieve a certain goal.

You will hardly finding a super model talking about how beautiful she is but almost all wannabees will keep talking about how beautiful they are because they are not yet sure that that they are that beautiful or that they are recognized for their beauty.

If you suddenly landed a good job that pays really well you might feel like wanting to show of in front of your friends to show them how brilliant you are but if you became a billionaire then you will rarely feel like wanting to show off your wealth.

So we can conclude that people also show off their wealth when they feel that they aren't well recognized or when they feel that their achievement is not big enough.

But we can be respected, admired, even followed without having those advantages (wealth and position) if we are able to manifest ourselves as a person with full of positive characters, right thoughts and good attitudes.

History has noted many people who successfully achieved high rank in society although they were poor and no position. You can see in history the life of Mahatma Gandhi, Confucius, Buddha, even Jesus Christ and the Prophet Muhammad (pbuh). They weren't wealthy people, handsome, and grabbed the position politically.

People always remember those names above untill this day. Their sermons always be heard, They gave inspiration for many people. Many books on them and their teaching have been published.

Confucius believed in the perfectibility of all men and he was against the idea that some men are born superior to others. During his time it was held that nobility was a quality determined by status and that belonging to a specific social circle made a person morally superior. Confucius challenged this idea by saying that being morally superior had nothing to do with the blood, rather, it was a matter of character and personal development, a revolutionary concept at that time. For that, Emperor Qin Shi Huang (Shi

Huangti, 259-210 BCE) banned Confucianism along with all other schools, except for the Legalist school or *Fa-jia*, which was the official government philosophy. Freedom of speech was suppressed, hundreds of Confucian scholars were buried alive and several classic Chinese texts were burnt.

Winning without degrading or humiliating others has been applied by the Prophet Muhammad (pbuh) when signing the Constitution of Medina or Madina Charter that unites Muslims and Clans in the Medina (including Jewish clans) in one society. Please pay attention to the following articles excerpted from Madina Charter's text:

16]. Those Jews who follow the Believers (who signed the Charter) will be helped and will be treated with equality. (Social, legal and economic equality is promised to all loyal citizens of the State).

17] No Jew will be wronged for being a Jew.

18] The enemies of the Jews who follow Us (The Believers) will not be helped.

As discussed in the previous chapter, when the Prophet Muhammad conquered Mecca, a city that used to be very hostile and expelled him, with a hundred thousand troops the Prophet Muhammad could have slaughtered the inhabitants of Mecca but he did not, instead he said :

"I speak to you in the same words as (Prophet) Yusuf spoke to his brothers. This day there is no reproof against you; Go your way, for you are free."

The Prophet called them (the Meccans) back home promising to forgive all their past assaults and guaranteed their protection. Mecca became a land of peace and serenity, thanks to his efforts and merciful invitation.

The Prophet's immense forgiveness is an example for us today as to how we should engage with past atrocities. It is a message of self-reformation that teaches us that we can subdue feelings of revenge and hatred and build a society in compassion and love.

The true victory is not just you managed to defeat the enemy, but the victory over yourself. When you defeated yourself, then the whole world will be bent over you. Trust me!

5

DO NOT EASILY TEMPTED BY ANYTHING GLAMOUR AND BEAUTIFUL, DO NOT QUICKLY CHANGE YOUR MIND IN ORDER NOT TO REGRET IN THE END
(AJA MILIK BARANG KANG MELOK, AJA MANGRO MUNDAK KENDO)

This philosophy reminds us to be firm and not easily shaken when face with several options, the beliefs that are not easily changed only because seeing something else that look better than the previous option. Because an appearance and casing are often deceptive, something that looks interesting from the outside is necessarily good and beneficial for us.

It has become the habit of majority people, they are very easily tempted by something looks good and beautiful. And most of them did not consider the quality, benefits, consequences, and its effects. Their interest based on viewing the physical appearance only. And in the end, remorse will be too late.

For example, someone who already has a good job then someday he quit from his office and get another job that he thought is better, more bigger salary and promising in the future. But he didn't think about whether his new job is adjust with his capability and skill, or if he would feel comfortable in his new office? After moving to the new office, he realized his mistake to change the job.

Another example, someone who is looking for a life partner. Many people had chooses their life partner carelessly and gave more priority to physical appearances or charm, muscular or sexy body. They didn't thought about partner's habits, moral, their behavior on a daily basis, and so on. They are so hurry and select their life partner carelessly, soon after the marriage, they will feel sorry and surprised that her partner is much different than before they were united. All of the veil that had previously covered the vices, will open and reveal the true face of our spouse, like "Romeo with Vampire Fangs."

Another example, a cheating and had a secret relationship because he/she looked his/her paramour was more handsome/beautiful than than his/her spouse. Such thinking is obviously not feasible, because just based on mere lust. not common sense.

We can see many more examples around us that give a lesson to decide carefully. Don't try to make decisions in a hurry. Don't make decisions when you're mad, sad, or frantic. Take time to calm down and consider everything rationally.

Many people are now vying to change their physical appearance in various ways but have one purpose: to be more beautiful or handsome. Among them there are willing to pay more to change the shape of their body or face.

As discussed in previous chapter on craving for status, wealth, and popularity, the obsession to look more beautiful or handsome is part of the misguided behavior that always wants to be appreciated, respected, and admired.

Many people's hearts become hard because they are too obsessed with looks, wealth, and luxury.

Why charm and physical appearance is so important to you? You are so concern with your body no matter what fills your soul, whether anger, hatred, or lust? Remember, a value of snail's shell doesn't change though its decorated nicely.

However, the main value of man does not depend on their bodies or faces, but rather depends on their souls, behavior, and moral. The values that make humans have a lasting name. Does Mahatma Gandhi a handsome or wealthy person? Do Confucius, Budha, Jesus, and Muhammad have those advantages?

If indeed they have physical charm or material advantage, obviously not those things that makes them so glorified and have many loyal followers.If any of them are filthy rich, even their wealth exhausted because it is used to spread the sacred values to others.

The Materialistic society tries to place measurable value on everything. It claims, "Everything has its price." Those of the world are constantly assessing the value of their *stocks, bonds, bank CDs, 401k, insurance policies, pension plans, welfare checks, food stamps, minimum wage, etc., etc.* They feel they must place some kind of material value on the human life or human soul.

There is more joy in pursuing less than can be found in pursuing more. In many ways, this is a message that we already know to be true. Just like Mae West (an American sexy actress), said:

"You only live once, but if you do it right, once is enough."

But since the day we were born, we have been told something different. We have been told that possessions are equal with joy, and because we have heard that so many times, we began to believe it. As a result, we spend our lives working long hours to have more money so that we can buy nice stuffs.

When (again) we hear the simple message that there is more joy in the things that are less than can be found in the pursuit of more things, this message was ringing in our hearts, because our hearts already know it's true. We knew that wealth does not necessarily mean joy and happiness. And we knew that life is too precious to waste in chasing of them.

It just helps to be reminded from time to time. So today, remember...

Our life is short. We only get one shot at it. The time goes by quick. And once we use it up, we can't get it back. So make the most of it. Possessions steal our time and energy. They require unending maintenance to be cleaned, maintained, fixed, replaced, and removed. They steal our precious attention, time, and energy and we don't even notice it... until it's too late.

Our life is unique. Our look, our personality, our talents, and the people who have influenced our lives have made us special. As a result, our life is exactly like no one else. And just because everyone else is chasing material possessions doesn't mean we have to too.

Our life is significant. Far more than success, our hearts desire significance because significance lasts forever. On the other hand, possessions are temporal. They perish, spoil, and fade. And most of them, by design.

Our life is designed to inspire. Let's make footprints worth following. Nobody ever changed the world by following someone else. Instead, people who change the world live differently and inspire others to do the same. Possessions may briefly impress, but they never inspire.

Our life is important. Our heart and soul makes us valuable. Don't sacrifice your important role in this world by settling for possessions that can be purchased with a card of plastic.

Our life deserves better. Joy, happiness, and fulfillment are found in the invisible things of life: love, hope, peace, and relationships. And they are not on sale at your local department store. Stop looking for them there. People who live their lives in pursuit of possessions are never content. They always desire newer, faster, or bigger because material possessions can never satisfy our deepest heart desires.

Be reminded that your life is far too valuable to waste chasing material possessions. And find more joy today by choosing to pursue "better" rather than "more."

6

DO NOT EASILY OFFENDED WHEN CALAMITIES BEFALL, DON'T BE SAD WHEN LOSING SOMETHING
(DATAN SERIK LAMUN KETAMAN, DATAN SUSAH LAMUN KELANGAN)

Life can be tough these days. It genuinely seems like we are stuck in a rat race – work is boring, family is difficult, you just can't find the social network and warm feeling of brother/sisterhood, and of course, you're still single. And then on top of all this, mum is not well and dad has passed away. This may resonate with a lot of you or parts of this may, and the consequences of all this are that many of us circumnavigate life through bouts of depression. *We feel a sadness that sometimes we do not know quite how to overcome.* We feel an anxiety that we have no idea what it stems from. Ultimately what we find is that despite all the pleasures of the world, we are still fighting a sadness, anxiety and a feeling of sorrow, which manifest in different ways.

When a Somebody encounters hardships, he must realize that it is a time for expiation of his sins, it is a promise for huge rewards by God for his patience and it is an instance of remembrance of God. These hardships carry glad tidings of forgiveness for the believers. The righteous predecessors use to be pleases on facing hardships, as this indicated their elevation of rank in Paradise and forgiveness from God.

A Believer should not forget that God doesn't burdens a person beyond his strength. In the holy Quran states *"Our Lord! Punish us not if we forget or fall into error, our Lord! Lay not on us a burden like that which you did lay on those before us (Jews and Christians); our Lord! Put not on us a burden greater than we have strength to bear. Pardon us and grant us Forgiveness. Have mercy on us. You are our Protector"* (Soorah Baqara. Verse: 286)

If every adversity or hardship time are not beyond our strength, please be patience and keep your faith on. Always ask God for forgiveness, strength, wellbeing, and help.

Panic and impatience cannot prevent the coming of problems. Complaining is contradictory to patience. Patience is not an easy behavior to gain. The Almighty has granted us several examples of patience shown by the Prophets during hard times. One of the most powerful of these narrations told to us by God is the one of Ayyub (Job in the Bible). There are many gems of wisdom in this story for a productive persons.

A scholar said: "To have patience means that one's common sense and religious motives are stronger than one's whims and desires." It is natural for people to have an inclination towards their desires, but common sense and the religious motive should limit that inclination. The two forces are at war: **sometimes reason and religion win, and sometimes whims and desires prevail. The battlefield is in the heart of man.**

Story of Prophet Ayyub (Job) shows us that he never complain or desperate. He even enjoying his adversity and hard life as prove of God's love.

When Ayyub loss his family, wealth and children, and he had nothing left, he started to focus upon the remembrance of God, and he said:

I praise You, the Lord of lords, Who bestowed His kindness upon me and gave me wealth and children, and there was no corner of my heart that was not filled with attachment to these worldly things, then You took all of that away from me and You emptied my heart, and there is nothing to stand between me and You. If my enemy Iblis knew of this, he would be jealous of me.

Praying in Adversity Strengthen Bond Between Man And God

The first category of trials and tribulations that I have mentioned above, arise when one accepts an appointee of God and the truth he stands for. Unfortunately, those who accept the truth are always few and lack numerical strength. Their opponents are greater in number, stronger, and bent upon their extirpation. It becomes necessary, in fact, there is an intense need for the ones who stand for the truth to ask for Divine assistance. Who is there besides God to help them? That is the reason why in the first verse in this lesson, God tells us to ask for His help, but show patience while doing so. Facing adversities with patience in itself evokes Divine assistance. It is part of human nature to ask for help, therefore God enjoins us to ask for His assistance through prayer and supplication. Patience is enjoined upon those who believe in the truth, so that the difficulties they have to face to uphold the truth, result in firmly anchoring the truth to their hearts. Truth becomes a part of their very essence, provided they face adversity, and remain steadfast in their belief. The reason such a person is permitted to ask for Divine help through prayer, and supplication is that it strengthens the bond between man and God. This bond becomes even more stronger with the prolongation of adversity. This is the greatest benefit of having to face difficult times. The purpose of truth is to establish a relationship between man and God. When man prostrates and cries before his Lord, the burden on his heart is lifted, and he eventually finds pleasure and exhilaration in doing so. This is the greatest blessing of this life, and the Hereafter.

If in spite of patience, and asking for Divine assistance, difficulties do not resolve, one should not take this as an indication that God is not with him, and that all his prayers were wasted. That is why Divine words of solace are repeated, "Surely God is with the patient." Therefore, one should keep up prayer, and remain patient thereafter.

Adversity Is A Means For Spiritual Development

The second category of adversities which man has to face are those which are ordained by God for mankind as his fate, meaning the Divine law or the measure of his growth, and development, or as a trial from Him. These occur in the form of fear, apprehension, hunger, poverty, or a loss of life, property, and the fruits of his effort. These trials are for the purpose of exposing the hidden condition of man's soul, both its weaknesses and its strengths. For example, if a person is involved in an adverse circumstance, and he lies, bribes, steals, or breaks a promise to get out of it, then this situation has made apparent for him the weaknesses that were hidden in his character. This provides for him an opportunity to reform himself before his life ends, and he has no other remedy for his spiritual illness, but the fire of hell. On the other hand, those who face these Divinely ordained measures of growth, and development with patience, their character evolves such qualities which were not there before, and their hidden potential is thus manifested. A tree which sheds all its leaves, and faces the harsh winter, bears flowers and fruits, in springtime. The good qualities which adorn the character of man, like fruits and flowers are the same which will form the pleasant fruits and flowers of the garden of eternity.

This is why it is stated:

"And give good news to the patient,"

i.e., those who face such trials with patience. As to what this good news is will be discussed later, but before this we are informed as to who the patient ones are. These, it is stated are the ones, who when faced with a Divinely ordained trial say, "Surely we are God's, and to Him we shall return." They admit that they belong to God, and that He may do with them as He pleases. The loss or damage, they may have suffered does not matter, for they have to return to their Lord, and if He is pleased with them, He will give them reward in the life Hereafter, which would be more than the loss they suffered. All the worldly possessions are eventually lost at the time of death. Our Ancestors then tell us that these are the people who in this very life receive the protection, and the blessings of God. What is this protection of God from? It is from one's misdeeds, weaknesses, negligence, and from their adverse consequences. It is also from the repetition of these acts, for there is always a danger of this. For example, if someone steals, it becomes easier for him to steal again. A patient individual, thus not only comes under the protection of God, but he is also favored with spiritual blessings from God. Spiritual blessings are the real blessings, for the worldly blessings either finish during, or certainly at the end of one's life. The spiritual blessings will, however accompany the spirit into the eternal life Hereafter, where the blessings will also assume an external palpable form.

7

DO NOT EASILY AMAZED, DO NOT EASILY DISAPPOINTED, DO NOT EASILY SHOCKED, DO NOT ACTED LIKE A CHILD

(AJA GUMUNAN, AJA GETUNAN, AJA KAGETAN, AJA ALEMAN)

Have you seen the phenomenon in our society, which is most of us belong to *"gumunan"* people or astonished and amazed easily. For example, when seeing a wealthy man who had luxury cars, or top entrepreneurs with assets that are scattered everywhere, and celebrity which is very handsome or beautiful. Among us there are people who astonished and amazed by all those things. Firstly, feeling amazed is a normal thing, but the problem is how do you manage that such feeling wisely, as long as it doesn't make you think short.

People who easily amazed at something or someone is the most suitable candidate to become fanatic followers. Their admiration will bring them to a narrow, bigot, and unbalance thinking, so their assessment are not objective anymore.

When looking at someone successful and have a luxury car, because of your admiration to him then you specify the criteria for happiness and success is to be like that person. Until you become obsessed in pursuing of all the wealth in order to become more successful like people you admire.

Since you've been obsessed, you will do anything to achieve it. No matter the rights of others, regardless of the feelings of others, as long as it is advantageous for yourself, you will do it!

If so, what's the difference between you and a boar that always searching for food in dirty and smell places?

Even when you've been amazed by someone, you'd be so easy to follow what he was doing, what he wears, and what he says. If the person you admired is a celebrity, then you will imitate his style and always looking for news about him. If that person is a religious figure, noble people, or a political leaders, then you've been a part of his "death squads".

You're not easy to accept if there is something bad befalls on the people you admire. You will very easily offended if they criticized or humiliated.

On the other hand, another meaning of "*Aja Gumunan* (Do not Easily Amazed)" is many people who experience culture shock. To put it simply, try to take a look at some people that suddenly so famous, wealthy, unexpectedly came to power in a country and so on. See and note if there is a drastic change in their attitude and behaviour? Such as their speaking style, clothes they wear, their dining places, the way they socialize, and so on. If there is a drastic change, then they were actually experienced a culture shock. Of course there is nothing wrong of it, because all of those are their choice. But however we must keep clever in positioning ourselves wisely.

"*Aja Getunan* (Do Not Easily Disapointed)", as human beings we should always be prepared to face the bad things that we are not expected. Because we are not able to predict everything, there are still things beyond our capacity as human beings. We will never be able to fight against His destiny. For example we're starting a little business by making the mobile shop, but then it burned or stolen unexpectedly. We lost the only business in life.

Disappointed and sad Yes. But disaster should not make us fall in deep regret of what happened, blaming the situation is not a correct attitude.

In this case, we are trained to be more sincere or gracefully. All things have it consequences and will definitely return to us. Well the bottom line is do not regret and disappointed easily when you are doing something positive. Even if you fail or suffer a disaster, don't ever stop in your positive efforts.

But as humans we can prepare and anticipate the worst possibilities to reduce the sense of regret. As once said by John Jay in 1813: "Hope for the best and prepare for the worst", it means You should have a positive attitude, but make sure you are ready for disaster.

While my father was in the hospital after his heart attack, we hoped for the best and prepared for the worst. When you study for a major exam, hope for the best but expect the worst. Don't make yourself anxious worrying that it will be too difficult, but a review of the u.s. if you expect the exam to be extremely hard.

But as humans we can prepare and anticipate the worst possibilities to reduce the sense of regret. As once said by John Jay in 1813: "Hope for the best and prepare for the worst", it means You should have a positive attitude, but make sure you are ready for disaster.

Preparing for the worst is tinged with despair, which is the opposite of hope. When you prepare for the worst, you are planning for something negative that may or may not happen. In order to prepare for the worst, you must look at your situation and love through the lens of despair. This vision keeps you from feeling hopeful and from focusing on your desired positive outcome.

This becomes a self-fulfilling prophecy of getting what you are focusing on – instead of the true and lasting love you desire, you get love that is fleeting. If you tend to live by the philosophy of *"hoping for the best and preparing for the worst"* you may find yourself saying something like, "It's a good thing I'm prepared for the worst."

The definition of hope is the state which promotes the desire of positive outcomes related to events and circumstances in one's life... Being hopeful is feeling that something you want may happen or things will turn out for the best.

Planning for the worst weakens whatever hope you have. And living with hope and despair will cause you to approach love with caution, uncertainty and fear.

If you don't want to be let down by hoping for the best or think you should be prepared for the worst so you can feel good when the worst doesn't happen, this can drain your energy. You don't have to live this way anymore.

"Aja Kagetan (Do Not Easily Shocked)", meaning we must learn to be introspective, vigilant and flexible. Because nothing is impossible in this world. Everything can still happen in your life. Never underestimate anyone. Be reasonable and wise.

But if we apply the principle of *"hoping for the best and preparing for the worst"* that fits in to philosophy *"Aja Getunan"* and *"Aja Kagetan"*, then surely you'll be able to minimize the bad risk. Thus, surely you would not easily surprised because everything was well prepared.

"Aja Aleman (Do Not Acted Like A Child)*"*, From these simple words, we can take a lessons that you, in this life, don't always like to be praised by others, do not always want to adored highly by others, do not always want to be the center of attention, and too much complaining. People who tend to be spoilt will exaggerate something that actually small and dismissive of something that really matters. We learn that this life must be fought with great tenacity, but also flowing flexibly and wisely.

Ahmad Dzikran

8

DO NOT IMPRISONED BY DESIRE TO ACQUIRE HIGH STATUS, WEALTH, AND WORLDLY SATISFACTION
(AJA KETUNGKUL MARANG KALUNGGUHAN, KADONYAN LAN KEMAREMAN)

When a man's heart becomes attached to a woman, even though she is lawful for him, his heart will be her captive. She controls him and manipulates him as she wills. In appearance he is her lord because he is her husband or her possessor. However, in reality, he is her captive and is possessed by her especially when she knows his need and his passion for her. Then she will control him in the same way in which a conquering, aggressive master controls an overpowered slave who cannot escape from his master. Even worse than this is the captivity of the heart; this is more severe than the captivity of the body, and enslavement of the heart is much more severe than the enslavement of the body. Verily, whoever's body is subdued, enslaved and captivated will not care so long as his heart is reassured and is serene. In this way, it is possible for him to escape.

The same is true for one who is seeking leadership and dominion on earth. His heart is a slave to those who help him with his aim although he, in appearance, is their leader and the obeyed one among them. In reality he has hope in them and fears them. He would offer them wealth and countries, and would overlook what they have wrongly committed so that they would obey and help him with his aims. In appearance he is an obeyed leader while in fact he is their obedient slave.

So as the one who strives for wealth; this wealth can tie and subdue him. However, wealth is of two types: one type is that for which the servant of God has a need, such as food, drink, shelter and marital life. This type should be asked for from God and should be sought for His pleasure. Thus, this wealth, which a person uses for his needs, is of the same level as his donkey which he rides, or his mat, on which he sits. Furthermore, it should be regarded on the same level as a water closet in which he satisfies his need without becoming subdued or dismayed by it. It was said:

"Irritable (discontented) when evil touches him and niggardly when good touches him."

The other type of wealth is that which servant of God does not need for his necessities. He should not attach his heart to this type of wealth. For if he does attach his heart to it, he becomes subdued by it. Furthermore, he might begin relying upon other than God. Then, nothing of the actual worship which is due to God nor of the true reliance upon God will remain with him. Instead, he will be pursuing a branch of worship of other than God and a branch of reliance upon other than God. This person is the most deserving of the saying of our ancestors:

"May the worshipper of money be wretched. May the worshipper

of money be wretched. May the worshipper of velvet cloth be wretched. May the worshipper of silk cloth be wretched."

This person is indeed a slave of these objects. For if he asks God for these objects and if God grants him what he has requested, then he is pleased. But if God denies him what he has asked for, he is upset. However, the true servant of God is the one who is pleased with what God and his Messenger. Loves and hates what is hated by God and his Messenger and will make allegiance with the companion of God (those near to God) and take for enemies the enemies of God.

One of the prevailing criteria of the world we are living now is the predominant desire of man toward material wealth. The world is dominated, mostly by the greed of man, translated in their obsession of material wealth. Money, as the symbol of extravagance and richness, has been the magic word of the modern man. Books on how to generate business, to maximize profit, and to become rich in the shortest possible time, pack the best-sellers shelves of every bookshop, hence accelerating the economic madness and material frenzy of the modern life. Every inch of human life is measured by dollars and cents, credit and debt, profit and loss. Man's own desire and greediness has become his new God while the phantom of his rapacity and selfishness turns out to be his new religion.

Man suddenly forgets the pertinent lesson from history that abundance of wealth so far is the best demolisher of human civilizations. We saw abundant wealth of the fallen Persian Empire including gold, silk, fine carpets and so on. When Khalif Omar saw those treasures, he suddenly wept. When asked about the reason of his sadness in that supposedly cheerful occasion, response, *"This abundant of wealth has been the cause of down fall of the Persian Kingdom, and now it come to us to indicate our downfall."*

The tendency of being swayed by the temptation of material wealth is indeed very strong in man. The love of wealth according to our ancestors is the everlasting inspiration for man to think that he will not leave the world: *"The children of Adam will definitely be getting old but two things in him that will be always young, his hope and his love of wealth."*

SPRITIUAL FREEDOM AS ULTIMATE GOAL

It may be clear at this point that a human being can easily lose their freedom as they become psychologically enslaved to the various non-material idols of this worldly life. And evidently, this can lead to disastrous psychological, social, moral and spiritual consequences. But is there another perspective of freedom that allows for human beings to attain that elusive freedom of the soul? Interestingly, a close examination of the Islamic teachings presents a moral paradigm of freedom that is worthy of our consideration.

From the Javanese traditional perspective, our lives are not meaningless, nor devoid of any ultimate purpose. ***"Do you think that We created you aimlessly and that you would not ultimately return back to Us?"*** So what then is the purpose of our lives? Our lives are a spiritual journey towards God, to deepen our relationship with Him. ***"O Human, indeed you are laboring painfully towards your Lord, but you shall surely meet Him."*** All the hard and painful experiences in life actually present opportunities for us to build ourselves as better human beings by building our relationship with God. If we transform these experiences into spiritual growth and development, we find true liberation and serenity. ***"The one who purifies his soul is successful"*** A human being is successful when he or she achieves the freedom of the soul, by strengthening its connection with the Divine and empowering it with moral virtue. When the soul becomes awakened to the reality of life, it is not distracted by obsession with materialistic pleasures, but instead it is galvanized to spread mercy and compassion, and become the very embodiment of moral virtue. Such a soul is truly free. It is free to see beyond the immediate gratification of desires and look instead towards what brings about the greatest good. As famously said, **"True wealth is not abundant riches. True wealth is the contentment of the soul."** Such a soul is free to recognize its incredible potential as a servant of God, capable of bringing unlimited good into the lives of others. Such a soul is emancipated from the shackles of worldly enslavement, and has the understanding of what is truly valuable in life. A soul that wants only to consume what is placed in front of it is not truly free. But a soul that sees all the options, that looks beyond what is immediately pleasurable, is a soul that is free to choose whatever brings about the greatest prosperity and spiritual welfare.

So let us return to one of our initial questions – what is true freedom? It should be clear from the foregoing discussing that a disproportionate focus on physical freedoms actually does not equate with true freedom, and in many cases it leads to a clear loss of psychospiritual freedom. True freedom in its most basic form then is the the awareness and clarity of mind to desire those things which lead to one's prosperity. This is a freedom that is cultivated when one's soul is awakened to the reality of life, and connected with the sources of spiritual purification. A soul that understands its purpose in life is free to focus on those things in life that truly matter, free to value substance over style, free to value meaningful relationships over superficial appearances – and most importantly, free to actualize one's full potential by developing the moral qualities that bring one closer to God.

Ahmad Dzikran

9

DO NOT FEEL THE SMARTEST IN ORDER NOT MISGUIDED; DO NOT LIKE TO CHEAT IN ORDER NOT TO TRAPPED IN MISFORTUNE
(AJA KUMINTER MUNDAK KEBLINGER. AJA CIDRA MUNDAK CILAKA)

A fraudster will consider themselves the most clever when he knows he's not so smart. He tried to beat others and always looking for weakness of others, then he acted like a great teacher and lecturer, make people bigot and believe him. After that, he will seek a benefit from his followers, just like a proverb says, *"a wise men's wisdom also learned by a fraudster."*

There is indeed such a person usually referred with the term "snob": i.e. the attitude of posing like a smart person. The cause of this attitude can be various, such as feeling shame if he deemed not knowing something, want to show other people that he knows and understands (though he just a know a little bit or doesn't know at all), wants to be considered as great person, and very scared if he is considered a fool, always want to beat your opponent of the dialogues, and the worse part is he always try to offend anyone who has a difference of opinion with him. There are certain people who have such mannerisms.

Usually, such person always want to be heard by others. Or if he writes something, he expected his opinion read by someone else. Thus he would get psychological satisfaction (which is false).

In General, a snob person also always feeling envious on others. He always does not like what is being said, written, made or owned by someone else. His mind was always negative and likes to denounce others. And he always felt more superior than others.

Such person usually having a psychological problem. It can be caused by anxiety, stress, psychological pressure or even abnormal personality. It is also can caused by incorrect way of thinking and that incorrectness continues. Or, he/her has a bad habit but he/her never realized.

The other character is reluctant to ask. For him, asking about something tantamount to indicate that he was stupid. Therefore he was reluctant to ask about something even though he's actually stupid or does not know anything. In order not to be considered a fool, then he speaks or writes as if he knows a lot of things. Whereas, for people who have much knowledge or extensive vision, certainly will easily find out that what was said or written that is incorrect.

The consequences is he cannot appreciate other argumentation or do not accept advise. He always view another opinions are wrong and always wrong. He often acted like a teacher to show that he was smart, imposing his opinion to others without any rational explanation.

Cheating Will Destroy You

One effects of cheating is the loss of honesty and sincerity to gain more benefits, either material or non material. Cheating will form the avarice on someone who will never be satisfied so he/she does everything including the sneaky way. That's Cheating.

Fraudulent and deceptive stance will eliminate mutual trust in public life. The fraternity broken and the loss of a sense of affection between fellow human beings which then cause destruction, selfishness, and want to win themselves, envy and greed.

From deceiving and cheating, someone may be gain more money or reach the top position in one company. But it will only take him/her into the darkness, his/her heart is going darker day by day. Plus the burden of bad reputation and humiliation from others. Those who maintain the good reputation of himself and his family, must avoid various forms of suffering emerging from the darkness of heart and humiliation. They will be wary of an intention to commit fraud and cheating. No matter how hard the job competition and the burden of life, that's no excuse for the wise to commit fraud and cheating. Only people who aren't grateful that doing the cheating, and finally destroy themselves.

Cheating in order to seize the possessions of others, or to take a position that should have been given to his partner, even it is still in the form of an intention in mind, it remains a crime. Yes, a crime that is very detrimental to himself. If this evil thoughts was realized into action, then crime is widespread increasingly by harming people who were deceived and cheated, and their families as well. Coupled with unrest caused in the wider community if the deeds of deception and cheating increasingly rampant.

If someone still has the intention to commit fraud and cheating, no matter how small it is, he still belongs to the bad guys, not the wise man. Because only evil people who have evil thoughts. Wealth as a result of acts of fraud and cheating might make your bank account grow. However, the wealth generated from the bad ways certainly will pose a very adverse impact for your own mental health, which will lose hope to live an enlightened, enjoying the true happiness in the gift of God's love. Someone who suffered devastation due to fraud and cheating by somebody else may be able to rise up and experienced the recovery again. But those who destroy other people by committing fraud and cheating will experience the devastation that will not be easy to recover. Amritanandamayi Devi (a Hindu spiritual leader and teacher) says, *"Beware, your actions determine your future."*

Although the cheating was done secretly, wrapped up neatly by a conspiracy, eventually it will be revealed by the very bright disclosure (so that there is no place left to hide). May be God let you to reach the highest place by cheating, so He can drop you with a very painful fall.

10

DON'T BE ARROGANCE WITH YOUR AUTHORITY, YOUR STRENGTH AND YOUR KNOWLEDGE
(AJA ADIGANG, ADIGUNG, ADIGUNA)

Adigang: somebody who believes in power actually he does not confident enough. He put the power, position, and authority over everything, even over himself. Like he was "occupied" by his position.

That's mean, more less, the power they believe will not stand long.

When you are in top position, both in business or politic, you should not rely on your power to act arbitrarily and arrogant.

A Javanese classic record contained categorization of rulers, it was said:

"This is why those who are in authority are of two groups: the scholars and the rulers. If they are upright, the people will be upright; if they are corrupt, the people will be corrupt."

"God does not punish the individuals for the sins of the community until they see the evil spreading among themselves, and while they have the power to stop it, do not do so."

A Bad leader will make worst impact to whole society. A country can collapse because of one person. They seem to perfectly fit with our classic description - *"When authority is given to those who do not deserve it, then wait for the Hour."*

In a hadith (no. 2942) reported in Sunan Abu Dawud by Abu Maryam al-Azdi, the Prophet Muhammad (pbuh) said:

If God puts anyone in the position of authority over the Muslims' affairs and he secludes himself (from them), not fulfilling their needs, wants, and poverty, God will keep Himself away from him, not fulfilling his need, want, and poverty.

Concurrently, your followers must provide you with sincere and impartial feedback, support you, and help you orient yourself toward the good.

Adigung: property, wealth, money is important, but it is not everything. Use money to facilitate your goodness to others, to support the life of the poor. Do not waste your life by pursuing more and more treasure but you can't enjoy it at all. Read Luke 16: 9 in the Holy Bible,

"I tell you, use worldly wealth to gain friends for yourselves, so that when it is gone, you will be welcomed into eternal dwellings."

Do not use your wealth to manipulate people, or everyone will leave you. Very ironic, your wealth are growing while you are losing your friends and family.

"So if you have not been trustworthy in handling worldly wealth, who will trust you with true riches?" (Luke 16: 11).

As the apostle Paul so aptly tells his protégé Timothy in a letter: "For the love of money is a root of all kinds of evil, and in their eagerness to be rich some have wandered away from the faith and pierced themselves with many pains" (I Timothy 6:10).

We are reminded that we never know when our live will end, therefore you have to enjoy your life at this moment, because the moment will come when you can't enjoy anything anymore.

Adiguna: do not get drunk with your knowledge, your cleverness, and how many academic titles you have.

Often in this life, we found some politicians use his insights spoke a lie to the public, or removing the words diplomatically to refuse what they had promised before.

We also find some scientists who used his knowledge to deceive the public, made a false statements in order to achieve scientific award, academical degree, or popularity.

The intelligence of thought, the tenderness of feeling, and firmness of the soul can be obtained from the diverse of life experiences. Anand Krishna said his book *The Javanese Wisdom :* **"This universe is a great university that unbeatable by man-made institutions. So do not be over pride, there are still many people who are smarter than us. Stay humble though you have a many academic titles."**

ARROGANCE CONCEALED THE TRUTH AND DENIED PEOPLE'S RIGHT

You are advised to be humble. Humbling yourself to God and to other people. **You should interact with the people with good manners while pride is considered extremely dispraised and pushes people towards disbelief in God.**

Arrogance is one of the greatest reasons for having disbelief in God and to reject what was said by Prophets, Philoshopers, and Wise People came with

Our ancestors said : *"Arrogance is to conceal the truth and deny the people's right."*

Meaning it is the same to that person, whether one returns to truth or any right from the rights which come to you. You don't humble yourself to accept it and you reject it and you belittle those that come to you with it. You deny that which he comes with and reject the truth he has.

Arrogance is not allowed from any angle, an ugly characteristic that God abhors. **He will not enter paradise whoever has in his heart an atoms weight of arrogance.**

Wage war against yourself from falling into arrogance. An evil characteristic leading one to disbelief, belittlement of people and rejecting the truth. This is why this wise one (Luqman) advised his son to not turn his face away from men full of pride. This so that he doesn't become arrogant towards people.

A person speaks to you while you are haughty turning away from him. Humble yourself. **You are a poor person, weak, created from earth, created from a sperm that is of little value, how can you be arrogant?!**

How can you be arrogant towards the people while you are in this state. Who are you?!

Then, if a thorn pierces you, you cry because of it, how can you be arrogant towards people?

It is obligatory upon the person to degrade himself if his soul becomes arrogant, haughty and he should remind it of how worthless and lowly it is and that from the most degraded of people are the arrogant ones.

There isn't anyone lowlier than an arrogant person and no one becomes arrogant except from a despicable trait and degraded character and soul.

Ahmad Dzikran

11

WHOEVER HAS A NOBLE ASPIRATION, HIS LIFE WILL BE GUIDED
(SAPA WERUH ING PANUJU SASAD PAGER WESI)

People everywhere are asking the questions; "What is the purpose of life?" and "Why are we here?" You might be amazed to learn, that our Javanese ancestors was providing clear and concise answers for these questions.

Most of those who reflect or think about life in any detail will consider and ponder these questions. There are as many different answers to these questions as there are people asking the questions. Some would hold that the purpose of life was to acquire wealth. Yet suppose they were to acquire millions of dollars, what then would they claim is their purpose after doing so?

If the purpose of life is to become wealthy, there would be no purpose after you achieved success as wealthy guy.

The fact is that when people approach their purpose here in this life from the aspect of only gaining wealth, after collecting the money they have dreamed of their lives loose purpose and then they live in restless tension suffering from a feeling of worthlessness.

How could wealth then be considered as life goal?

Could the acquisition of wealth guarantee happiness? Of course not.

When we hear millionaires or members of their families committing suicide, how could we consider the purpose of life would be to gain great wealth?

A child of 5 years would obviously prefer a new toy to a deposit slip for a million dollars. A teenager does not consider millions of dollars in the bank a substitute for movies, videos, pizza and hanging out with his friends.

A person in their 80s or 90s would never consider holding on to their wealth in place of spending it to hold on to or regain their health.

This proves that money is not the main purpose at all the stages of one's life.

Wealth can do little or nothing to bring happiness to one who is a disbeliever in Almighty God, because regardless of what he or she would gain in this life they would always live in fear of what will happen to them in the end. They would wonder what would become of them and how they would end up.

Wealth and its accumulation as a purpose would be doomed to a temporary success at best and in the end it would only spell out self destruction.

So, what is the use of wealth to a person without belief? He would always fear his end and would always be skeptical of everything.

He may gain a great material wealth but he would only lose himself in the end.

All along, we are used to determine the material goals in our life, and consider it as the only purpose and term for life achievement.

But we never specify any non material purpose, a more abstract and spiritual purpose. Whereas this non-material purpose is more valuable and can guide you in this life.

For example, you have a purpose in life to make other people happy. Whether it's your family, elderly people, or the poors. Then when you have a lot of money, that money will be used to fulfil your life goal. Your life will be filled with sharing and caring. Because, by making other people happy, then your soul became happy and satisfied as well.

Even when you are in a top position as a political elite and leaders, the authority you have will be used to please others. You will become a leader who serves the people. Not a leader who always like to be respected and honored.

Materialistic goal of life caused by the point of view that life is only once, there is no life after we die. Never believe abstract, spiritual, and unseen things. But life is always in pairs: men and women; world and afterlife; physic and metaphysic; material and spiritual.

Ancient great societies based their beliefs on non material and spiritual values as highest goal. Ancient Egypt society believes the existence of life after death, the great viking warriors determined Valhalla (great hall for the deaths) as their purpose to fight and die.

But now the spiritual beliefs were destroyed in modern times. Humans believe that life is just once, there is no afterlife. All created from a natural process without any role of God as The

Only One Creator.

As a result of materialistic life goal: the man believes this life should be enjoyed, for we live just once, we should enjoy it by partying, dating with a lot of girls, drinking, accumulate wealth and much more.

Not all things in life this should and could be rationalized. Do you have to die first to simply prove that right there is life after death? Do you have to die first to make sure that heaven and hell are really exist?

This life is a test. A test of how you utilize your time. How you use your wealth? And how you use the power you have?

The time you have, do you use it to improve yourself, to learn something new, or to do good to other people? Or you use it to play around with, dating with many girls, collecting wealth?

Do you always collecting and calculating your wealth? Or is there just a little of it that you give to the poor?

If you are a leader, do the power you have you use it to serve people, or to trick and fool them?

This life is like a super competitive school or education. For example in U.S Navy Seal, promotion never comes in the U.S. Navy Seal program until you have been tested sufficiently to prove that you can be **trusted.** Your commanders and teammates need to know they can trust you, and you need to know which of them you can trust as well. Your instructors, your commanders, your teammates need to be absolutely convinced that you will give your life for the "cause" if forced to do so.

Character is both developed and revealed by tests, and all of life is a test. You are *always* being tested. God constantly watches your response to people, problems, success, conflict, illness, disappointment, and even the weather! He even watches the simplest actions such as when you open a door for others, when you pick up a piece of trash, or when you're polite toward a clerk or waitress.

When you understand that life is a test, you realize that nothing is insignificant in your life. Even the smallest incident has significance for your character development. Every day is an important day, and every second is a opportunity to deepen your character, to demonstrate love, or to depend on God.

This world is the place of striving and the Hereafter is the place of reward or punishment. Victory and success cannot be achieved except after tests which will bring the good forth from the evil and tell the believer apart from the disbelievers.

How to understand that this life is a test? By changing your point of view, start to believe that life is not just once. We live in this world, then we will die and resurrected again.

Life after death is the eternal life, this is the true life that supposed to be desired and pursued by a man. Because if we are happy in this second life, then it would be eternal. On the contrary, if we suffer in this second life, then you will never find the end.

So the view that life is only once and there is no life after death is a fallacy. Start change your old thinking, so you do not experience eternal regret later.

If you have right goal in this life, then you are walking on the right path, *SASAD PAGER WESI* (as if you had a lot of strong iron fences that guarding you from any possible danger).

12

PROBLEMS IN THIS LIFE IS NOT A BARRIER, BUT YOUR PATH TO PERFECTION

(ALANG-ALANG DUDU ALING-ALING, MARGINING KAUTAMAN)

We all come across various difficulties in our lives. However, not all of us handle them as effectively as we should. As strategies for getting through life's problems are rarely formally learned, we are constrained to use trial and error, sometimes leading to suboptimal results.

Dealing effectively with our difficulties and problems requires appropriate emotional control, acceptance of realities, charting out a course of action, and finally taking preventive measures to keep future problems at bay. Thus, arming ourselves with the right intellectual, mental, and spiritual strategies to get through these phases can help us achieve successful breakthroughs.

But, once again, your ability to face difficulties and problems depend on your view towards life. If you are an adherent of materialism, then you would not trust what is in this book, because this book invites to spiritualist thought.

Understand everything not only based on rationality, but use your heart, sharpen your heart and your feeling in order to catch hidden messages in any difficulties you face. In fact, the difficulty can be a very good means for you to have a very sharp heart.

Every difficulty definitely has a plus value, especially for yourself. God wants you to modify every difficulty and burden into a positive energy that drives the turbine within yourself in order to move faster, instead silent or retreat.

Once you successfully climb the cliff, then at the top you will find the beautiful landscape, the cool air that fully refreshing your soul.

We can read the journey of earlier people when they found difficulty, perhaps bigger than yours. Let's think about the journey of holy people, such as the prophets, they experienced hardship with great patience and strength soul.

Why Prophet Joseph have to go through the hardship first? He was exiled by his brothers into an old well, then he becomes a slave. Why Moses should be saved into a basket and placed into the river Nile?

Actually they were all being prepared, strengthened, so when the time came they will be ready to accept the revelation and take big mandate as prophets.

From here we can learn that the Prophets experienced hardship and difficulties because they will receive a greater task : prophetic mission. A sacred mandate that raised their level and purify them, glorify them over other human beings.

And there is no difference in the context of life among us with the prophets, except in the weight of the test, responsibility, and the revelation. As human, we have same potential with them to achieve higher values after we got through all difficulties in life.

In substance, we face all the hardships and difficulties are to prepare and to strengthen us, so that we can accept one another gifts much larger someday. What is it? All depends on how you go through difficult phases in your life.

One story is about the Kansas City Star who has fired a young Walt Disney because, according to his editor, he lacked imagination and had no good ideas. Another one says he delivered the newspaper as a boy and applied multiple times to work for the Star for jobs as cartoonist, office boy and driver but was turned down each time. As a young man, Disney went on to file for bankruptcy protection several times and overcame numerous obstacles while creating the Disney empire beloved by children and adults today.

When he was seeking funding for Disneyland in Anaheim, California, it's said that Disney was turned down by 302 bankers before he got the funding he needed. He prevailed, and Disneyland opened in 1955. Although Walt Disney did not live to see the 1971 opening day of Disney World in Florida, he would likely be pleased with the Disney company's continuing accomplishments, which included buying ABC, which in turn owned the Kansas City Star.

Failure after failure, Disney did not give up. Walt Disney kept pushing the envelope and consistently pursued what he knew he was capable of doing. Rather than focus on the past, he put his attention to the achievements of the future. This is what made his story such a legendary tale.

Walt Disney Animation House was Disney's "revelation" given by God to lift him and made him honoured by people in this world.

Then let'see the story of JK Rowling, one of success author in the world, it was said that Harry Potter book rejected 9-12 times. After spending six years writing the first installment of her "Harry Potter" novels, Rowling was rejected by 9 publishers before London's Bloomsbury Publishing signed her on.

She told another fan on Twitter that she received "loads" of rejections before she finally got published – Little sent the manuscript to 12 different publishers before it ended up with Bloomsbury.

"The first agent I ever queried sent back a slip saying 'My list is full. The folder you sent wouldn't fit in the envelope," replied Rowling. "I really minded about the folder, because I had almost no money and had to buy another one," says Rowling.

Now, Harry Potter sold at least 450 million copies all over the world. Her achievement is "sacred revelation" from God, made her life better and happy.

So, why you stopped? Why you turned back? Let's continue, achieve your dream although there are many barriers in your path. Achieve your perfection, take "revelation" from God.

Notice what Disney's said below:

"All our dreams can come true, if we have the courage to pursue them"

EMOTIONAL RESPONSE

An emotional response to a difficulty or calamity is normal and only human. However, emotions have to be managed and channeled appropriately; else they can manifest negatively within our personalities and affect our lives in general. Research, too, confirms that emotionally-reactive individuals confronting even relatively minor challenges in their lives are prone to increased physical problems and diseases.

One potential way people channel their emotions is to act them out uncontrollably and irresponsibly. In such situations, the prophet (peace be upon him) instructed us to exercise patience and to maintain a composed demeanor instead.

In other cases, emotions are channeled to fester, which then leads to the development of a victimized mindset. You may not realize it, but believing that your life is a teary saga may be the anchor weighing you down and preventing you from moving forward.

So, be conscious of how you channel your emotions. You can temper them with positive thinking and a strong faith. If you show any signs of having a victimized mindset then you need to snap out of it and adopt a more positive and reality based mindset instead. That can put you on the right path to get out of your difficulties faster.

TRYING TO MAKE SENSE OF THE DIFFICULTIES

The divine decree: When facing difficulties, our weak hearts can sometimes drive us to question the fairness of it all. In this context, we should remind ourselves that believing in God's Will and Decission.

As part of that belief, we should therefore recognize that God does what He wills for reasons that are only known to Him. Any attempt to comprehend with our limited minds His wisdom, or to understand how our current situation fits in His overall plan can only lead us to erroneous conclusions.

The "If-Only" Trap: Another trap that many of us fall into has to do with using the "if-only" logic. Very often, our minds tell us that "if I could have done such and such, then this wouldn't have happened." Our ancestors warned us against falling into such satanic traps. In a narration that said :

"……..If anything befalls you, do not say 'If only I had done (such and such), the such and such would have happened,' rather say: 'God has decreed and what He wills He does,' for 'if only' opens the door to the work of the shatan."

God's decrees is inevitable. Any attempt to imagine a different outcome based on different actions that we could have taken in the past will only increase our frustrations. This belief is also a blessing because it prevents us from returning to the past that can result in nothing but an added emotional baggage.

In this context, many among us also resort to blaming people, including those close to us. This blaming attitude in turn nurtures a mindset where people (even within families) resist future temptations to recommend anything or engage in an open dialogue. This not only weakens communications amongst people but also causes irreparable rifts and a loss of trust between them.

To summarize, accepting the divine decree can help us in not only forgoing the past but to also win God's pleasure. Suppressing our urge to blame others by maintaining a positive mindset can help us maintain healthy relationships and in also keeping good recommendations and advice flowing.

GETTING YOURSELF OUT OF TROUBLE

Having accepted God's decree, and after getting over any emotional challenges, the next step involves taking the right actions to get us out of our problems and difficulties. Actively engaging our God gifted faculties to pull us out of such situations is not as common as one may think. Thus, many a time we fail to achieve successful breakthroughs because we either follow a haphazard approach to resolve our problems or give up on our efforts too early in the process. This leads us to get stalled and makes us regard situations as irresolvable, hoping and praying for miracles to pull us out.

If you find yourself in such situations, this may be the time to rethink your overall approach. You see, most of us are accustomed to looking for "silver bullet" types of solutions. However, such solutions aren't that many and thus can't be relied on to get you out of your life's challenges. Adopting a realistic but methodical approach instead has a better chance of putting you closer to your desired outcomes.

This requires that you take time to define the problems and difficulties that you face with increased clarity and specificity. This is bound to yield better results because you will get clearer about the outcomes that you desire. You will also be able to clearly delineate the constituent tasks that potentially can put you closer to your desired solution. Follow those tasks through to the end with perseverance and patience and you may reduce the load of your problems.

On the spiritual front, we should recognize that if God puts us through trials or punishes us because of our sins or our bad attitude, the decision is His. However, as highlighted in another post on this site, seeking forgiveness through repentance can help undo the damage of our sins.

PREVENTIVE MEASURES

Finally, although God's decree is ordained, there are things we can do before hand to influence the outcome of our efforts, and thus prevent problems from piling up. First, we should never forget that God has provided us with a free will and associated faculties to think and act. As the prophet had stated, while we should fully trust God, we should tie our horse first – meaning we should use all our God-gifted faculties and exercise the required due diligence.

Second, for cases in which we fumble to choose between options, we should seek advice from God. By doing so, you consciously put your faith in Him to guide you. This will reduce the likelihood of you ending up with a failed outcome and thus an added burden for you to carry in the future.

To summarize, remember that effectively channeling your emotions, letting go of a negative past, maximizing the use of your God-gifted faculties, and above all a strong faith can help you attain the wisdom that life demands from you to get through even the most difficult challenges. Just ensure that you get serious about resisting the old attitudes and inculcate a positive mindset to propel you forward.

EPILOGUE : HUMAN'S PARADOX

We have higher and higher buildings, but getting lower our resistance to anger. We built many highways, but our insight is getting narrower. We spent a lot of money, but only a little we got. Lots of shopping, but the less that can be enjoyed.

More bigger home, but smaller family. More comfortable house, but we have no time to enjoy it. More elegant house, but chaotic family. More relations, but we have only a few neighbor. This is the time for double income, but divorces increasing are as well.

We have many academic titles, but our logic narrowed. More knowledge, but can't distinguish what is right and what is wrong. More scholars, and more problems. More medicines produced, but declining health.

We smoke and drink too much, too often, laughing too often, easy to angry, troubled sleep, reading too little, lazy to contemplate, watching TV too much and praying very rarely.

We've doubled our desire, but reduce ourselves values. Too much talking and less willing to listen. Too little love, and hate too often.

We have learned how to make a living, but not seeking the meaning of life. We are able to add years to our lives, but failed to bring life in the years of our lives.

We did great things, but failed to do good things. We cleaned the air, but our soul are full of pollution. We've conquered the atom, but do not able to defeat prejudice and envy. Too much judging, but less introspection.

We wrote a lot, but we learned a little. We have many plans, but little of them had been applied. We learn to catch, but did not learn to wait.

This is the era of fast food and slow digestion. Humans are physically larger, but has dwarfly character. This is the era of fast trips, disposable clothing, wasted morality, overweight bodies, and pills that can do everything: make you happy, soothing, beautifying and simultaneously kill you!

This is the time when many of the things exhibited and less that is stored. Remember, the real life is not measured by how much breath we take. But, it measured by the last breath we are.

This is the time when many things were exhibited, but less things we already saved. Remember, the real life is not measured by how much breath we take. But, it measured by the last moments of our breath.

ABOUT THE AUTHOR

Ahmad Dzikran is a freelance architect, web designer, writer in Indonesia, and has written dozens of articles and several books in Indonesia on religions, politic, social and history. This title is his fourth ebook published on the net. Other titles are : *The Compilation of Wisdom, The Christmas Wisdom, Wisdoms of the Legends.*

Now he is preparing some ebooks about wisdom, local myths, and symbolic architecture in Indonesia.

You can find more about me or my ebooks by visiting website : www.digitalbooks.id

or contact me by email : dzikran@digitalbooks.id, and follow my twitter : @ahmaddzikran

AVAILABLE SOON

These ebooks will be available soon. Just visit my site for more information : www.digitalbooks.id

1) THE WISDOM OF BALI (*INDONESIAN WISDOM SERIES #2*)

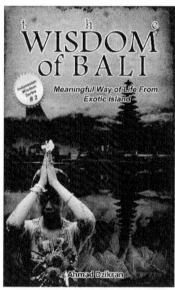

Bali, *Indonesia*. One of the exotic island, which is the only island that is predominantly Hindu. The Balinese traditional values contains a lot of meaning, guidance, and wisdom that are substantially universal, beyond time and space.

You may only see Bali in terms of uniqueness, their beauty of dance, clothings, and rituals. But you did not dug deeper the philosophy that underlies all of it.

Therefore just wait for the presence of this ebook soon, and get the enlightenment.

2) THE SUNDANESE WISDOM (*INDONESIAN WISDOM SERIES #3*)

The Sundanese (West Java, Indonesia) is often associated with the Sunda Land myth and high civilization of Atlantis that claimed by Arysio Santos was the sunken Sunda shelf.

The Sundanese are an agrarian society. They are very friendly, harmonious, and had a high kinship. They also have a number of traditions, symbolism, and philosophical values that keep them harmony with nature and human beings.

Now the Sundanese people are struggling to maintain their tradition, philosophy, and way of life from invasion of modern culture. This ebook is one way to introduce and to maintaining the wisdom values of Sundanese people so that more people in the world will understand and love their noble values.

Printed in Great Britain
by Amazon

81995136R00071